THE FORGING OF OUR CONTINENT

THE FORGING OF OUR CONTINENT

by CHARLTON OGBURN Jr.

Consultant
WILLIAM G. MELSON
Associate Curator, Department of Mineral Science
Smithsonian Museum of Natural History

Published by **AMERICAN HERITAGE PUBLISHING CO., INC.**
in association with **THE SMITHSONIAN INSTITUTION**

Book trade and institutional distribution by
D. VAN NOSTRAND COMPANY INC.

COVER AND FRONTISPIECE:
Rocks become granules; granules compact into rock again. Polarized light and extreme magnification illuminate, in grains of sand, the intermediate stage of the geologic cycle from rocks to sediments to rocks again. BELOW, *a U.S. Geological Survey team of the 1890's, one of the many such Government-organized parties that provided early knowledge of the history of our continent, stands atop a glacial moraine in the Alaskan panhandle.*

CONTENTS

THE
ANCESTRAL
ROCKS

On the northern side of Lake Superior is a country of rocks and ridges rising from a filigree of lakes and rivers. It is a country clothed in a forest dark with spruces and firs and veined white and pale grey-green with the trunks of canoe birches and poplars. Westward the hills run out in the Mesabi Range of eastern Minnesota, but the forest extends almost to the North Dakota line, giving way gradually to the prairie. (In Canada it rounds the prairies on the north and goes all the way to the Pacific.) Parts of it are rich in metals—silver, gold, copper, nickel—and from the Mesabi (the word means "great" in Chippewa) has come the equivalent of one ton of iron ore for every man, woman, and child on earth, leaving a desert landscape of man-made mesas and canyons.

But more than for the mineral wealth of the region, more even than for its frequently spectacular natural beauty, the northern shore of Lake Superior warrants special attention. The long hills that come down to the water or march out into it in promontories or islands are remnants of the oldest highlands of our continent and are formed of its oldest rocks.

The hills look ancient, especially the many with rock faces showing through the forest and those with palisades of rock like headbands just beneath their summits. The ledges of rock look ancient too, weathered grey and worn smooth as if by eons of surf. Some have veins of harder rock standing out on their surface like the veins on the back of a man's hand. Many are grooved with shallow, parallel furrows in a way that puzzled our forebears when they en-

Along portions of the Great Lakes lie the oldest rocks of the continent.

Fossils of organisms that lived earlier than the Cambrian period (500 to 600 million years ago) are rare, and so the geologic record of Precambrian rocks remains obscure. In 1910, Charles Walcott, then Secretary of the Smithsonian, uncovered the 500-million-year-old trilobite at left, one of the oldest ever discovered. This remarkably clear specimen predates the fish fossil below (from the Eocene epoch) by more than 400 million years.

countered the same phenomenon in the rock ledges of New England.

But ancient as they look, to appreciate just how very ancient these rocks and hills are is beyond human capacity. A life span is perhaps the maximum length of time for which we have a feeling. And seventy years, conceived in terms of hours as long as those we have spent in waiting rooms watching the hand of a clock creep imperceptibly forward, is a very long stretch indeed. It would take more than sixteen lifetimes to get us back to Charlemagne, which may not sound like a great deal, but it is ten million waiting-room hours—more than we can imagine. To return to the birth of civilization would take about 150 lifetimes. One hundred times as many would be required to put us back to the dawn of mankind and at the beginning of the series of eruptions that raised the line of volcanic cones crowning the Cascade Mountains of the Pacific Northwest, of which Mount Rainier, Mount Hood, and Mount Shasta are the most renowned. And that was an event of only yesterday in the history of the continent. To be on hand for the building of the Cascade Range itself we should have to go back over thirty times further still.

To see the birth of the Rocky Mountains fully under way we should have to go back some sixty million years—the time it would take a snail traveling at an inch a minute to encircle the globe twenty-four thousand times. And we should then be only at the latest of the major eras, the Cenozoic ("recent life" in Greek). Still, mammals would be replacing the dinosaurs, those extraordinarily successful reptiles

that reigned for twice as long as their warm-blooded successors have so far.

The Rocky Mountains, though senior to the Alps of Europe, are a fairly young range. The Appalachians are an old one—as human beings reckon things, that is. To get back to the time of their maximum development we must return to the start of the Mesozoic (middle-life) era, which preceded the Cenozoic and lasted twice as long as the Cenozoic has up to now. Dinosaurs would not have appeared, but the long, long era of the trilobites is at an end. Amphibians and early reptiles occupy the land. In other words, we are already well along in vertebrate evolution and not, even as life goes, very far back in the past after all.

The first vertebrates were fishes. These emerged rather early in what is known as the Paleozoic (early-life) era, which was almost twice as long as the Cenozoic and Mesozoic eras combined. As the geologists have divided time the first subdivision of the Paleozoic is the Cambrian. Much is heard of the Cambrian and Precambrian times; the reason is that the start of the Cambrian period—looking backwards—is the jumping-off place, since virtually no fossils have come down to us from earlier times. Rocks older than the Cambrian in which fossils might occur have, for the most part, been so thoroughly altered by processes of deformation that any fossils they might have contained would have been obliterated. For the rest, it is argued that living creatures of the Precambrian generally lacked the hard parts that lend themselves to fossilization. In any case, between 500 and 600 million years ago the fossil

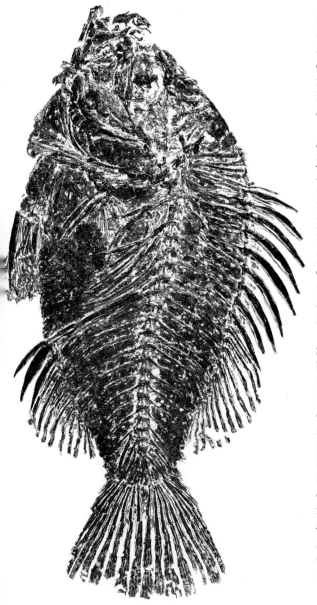

record ends, depriving geologists of an invaluable tool for determining what happened how and when. Only in recent years, with the discovery of methods of dating rocks according to the rate at which certain radioactive elements disintegrate, has light been thrown upon the hitherto dark ages preceding the Cambrian.

In the language of the geologists, "Precambrian" is an expression often heard in conjunction with "basement." All continents have a Precambrian basement, as it is called. The term signifies a floor of rocks that took form before the beginning of the Paleozoic era and have remained unaltered since then, except by being worn down where they have been exposed or by being uplifted where a bulge in the earth's crust has taken place locally. Rocks that have come out of the crucible, their minerals fused under heat and pressure, are dense, hard, and resistant.

In North America the ledges north of Lake Superior, to which we are working our way back, are an exposed portion of a Precambrian basement that constitutes the surface rock of the whole northeastern quarter of the continent, comprising an area of two million square miles in eastern Canada, northern Minnesota, northern Wisconsin, and northwestern Michigan. This elevated portion of the basement is known as the Canadian Shield, being comparable to a broadly convex shield lying face up. To the south and west of the Shield area, the stable platform of ancient rock slopes gently downward to pass beneath ever-thickening layers of younger formations that make up most of the surface rock of the United

OLYMPIC
MTS.

COAST RANGES

Willamette R.
PUGET-WILLAMETTE LOWLANDS

CASCADE RANGE

COLUMBIA

Columbia R.

BLUE MTS.

PLATEAU

ROCKY MOUNTAINS

NORTHERN ROCKY MTS.

CENTRAL ROCKY MTS.

SNAKE RIVER LOWLANDS
Snake R.

KLAMATH
MTS.

Sacramento R.

SIERRA NEVADA

San Joaquin R.

GREAT
SALT
LAKE

WASATCH RANGE

Green R.

WYOMING
BASIN

BASIN

DEATH VALLEY

ZION
CANYON

BRYCE
CANYON

GRAND
CANYON

PAINTED
DESERT

COLORADO
PLATEAU

MOHAVE DESERT

Colorado R.

TRANSVERSE RANGES

SALTON
SEA

AND

UPPER GILA MTS.

RANGE

PENINSULA RANGES

PROVINCE

GREAT

Yellowstone R.

Big Horn R.

BIG HORN RANGE

LARAMIE RANGE

FRONT RANGE

SOUTHERN ROCKY MTS.

SANGRE DE CRISTO MTS.

BADLANDS

BLACK
HILLS

PLAINS

Arkansas R.

Pecos R.

Rio Grande R.

THE GEOLOGIC PROVINCES OF THE UNITED STATES

States and western Canada—most of which is, of course, covered by soil. The Shield probably extends eastward and southward as far as the continental shelf beneath the waters of the Atlantic. Recently an oil company drilling at Cape Hatteras, North Carolina, brought up a core of it from nearly two miles down. On the other side, it presumably extends to the western margins of the Rocky Mountains. It may be seen at the bottom of the Grand Canyon, where it is less than a mile below the surface, only because there the earth's crust has domed up. Elsewhere these basement rocks have been thrust aloft in mountain-rearing upheavals, notably in the Adirondacks, the highlands of western New England, the eastern Appalachians and Piedmont, the Ozarks, the Black Hills, and the Rockies.

We expect rocks to look their age, and those of the basement do so where they have been long exposed, as in the Lake Superior region. The outcrops of the Canadian Shield that are encountered first in traveling eastward across northern Minnesota remind you of whales up from primordial depths of time. But the monotone grey, lichen-crusted surface of these monoliths is deceptive. Immediately beneath there is color and sparkle. Where the hillsides have recently been cut to make way for the highway that skirts the lake, the rock walls make you think of particolored desserts. (The cut has to be a new one, for rock quickly grows dull with exposure.) There are formations entirely of an arresting, deep-pink rock—pink granite, as it happens. More commonly, there are juxtapositions of great slices of near-black rock, gun-metal rock, old-rose rock, rock like grey loaf-sugar marbled with white or laced with wavy bands of white or pink like a pastry, and bologna-colored rock, and near-white or grey rock sequined with black crystals. In some cuts red-brick and putty-colored strata, bent and angled, alternate. For miles the flat sides of rocks that have split along cleavage planes are a chartreuse green or a darker green, as if they had been painted. To be exposed to such astonishing displays and remain indifferent to rocks and without curiosity as to their origins would seem to be all but impossible.

The most recent accession to the Canadian Shield of which we have knowledge was in the so-called Grenville province, a belt two or three hundred miles wide extending along the north side of the St. Lawrence and across Labrador to the coast. There, in the neighborhood of a billion years ago, rose a mountain range, of which the Adirondacks today form an outriding remnant elevated into mountains by a local uplift long after the original peaks had been worn down to the semblance of toothless gums. Presumably the formation was a mighty one in its era, ascending to heights equivalent to those of the Alps today but more forbidding than any range ever seen by man, for no vegetation relieved the severity of its slopes. Bare rock, jagged and ominous, rising from snowfields, with deserts of gravel where high meadows and forests would stand today, the terrain plantless and soilless to the ocean's edge —that was the Grenville range.

And yet when we have traversed the billion years that lie between us and the Grenville range, we are less than halfway back to the ancestral mountains of those diminished hills north of Lake Superior. They stand at a distance from us of something like 2.5 billion years. In the virtually endless duration of time through which this Archean range held sway such life as there may have been on earth was confined to the sea and was of the simplest kind. The winds that swirled among these summits were not of air as we know it but probably of gases of nitrogen, ammonia, and methane which would have asphyxiated any animal life in minutes. Yet the rise of the Grenville range was unimaginably distant in the future when the rock of one of the outcrops in Minnesota was formed. A sample of this rock has recently been determined to be 3.6 billion years old. It is a gneiss and, as such, a fragment of a mountain composed of minerals from yet more ancient mountains reconstituted in new form after an interval of tens of millions of years.

So this gneiss—a pink one—is itself the heir of still further reaches of time. When we arrive at the period when it originated we are indeed a very long, long way back in the past. According to recent findings reported by the Carnegie Institution, we are within about a billion years of the earth's beginnings—that is to say, from the time the raw materials of the planet were consolidated and fused into rock by the gravitational energy of their compaction and by heat from the disintegration of radioactive elements within the earth.

Scientists are working on the ages that preceded the Paleozoic (that is, Precambrian), analyzing rocks of the "Huronian series" of more than 1.4 billion years ago, of which the iron-rich taconite of the Mesabi Range is part, as well as "Keewatin lavas" and "Algoman granites," which go back perhaps 2.5 billion years. But from a history of the continent that commences with the Precambrian basement already fully formed, as it was perhaps 800 million years ago, we gain about as much understanding of its present forms as we could from one going back three times as far. However, there is one fact about the origin of the continental basement—or, more accurately, one presumption—that has an important bearing on what follows.

Except for that quarter that is designated the Canadian Shield, the basement is, as we have seen, buried beneath younger deposits thousands of feet thick, consisting of the wastage of ancient highlands or of minerals secreted by multitudes of marine organisms when the sea crept inland to the edge of the Shield. Few of the basement rocks beneath them will ever be seen by human eyes—though millions of years hence they may be raised and, stripped of their cover, laid bare once more beneath the sky. But, seen or unseen, it seems safe to say that from end to end the Precambrian basement is composed of the foundations of mountain belts originally resembling the youthful ranges of today and subsequently, by the agents of time, planed down to rolling hills. The history of our continent, as of other continents, is primarily the history of the rise and decline of mountains. And what mountains are is rock. Everything in the story of geology goes back eventually to rocks.

THE CYCLE
OF CONTEST

Rocks are combinations of minerals. And minerals are substances found in nature (not laboratory-made) that are inorganic (that is, not formed as parts of "organized" bodies, plant or animal) and that take definite, characteristic form in accordance with their internal atomic structure. That is to say, they are crystalline. Salt crystals, ice crystals, quartz crystals in sand, and crystalline gemstones are typical. (Etymologically, minerals are anything that is mined.) Minerals in turn are compounds of elements—exceptions being those that consist of a single element—and, generally speaking, of comparatively few: 98 per cent of the earth's crust is composed of only ten of the more than one hundred known elements. However, these elements in forming their compounds can behave in devilishly complicated ways.

The resourcefulness of elements in forming combinations has led to a rapidly growing popular interest in mineralogy. How many thousands of rock collectors there are would be hard to say, but their numbers must be great to account for all the rock-collecting clubs, the proliferation of publications on the subject, and the number of home-based dealers in rocks one discovers in traveling across the country. To account for the phenomenon there is the fascinating variety of minerals—twenty-five hundred by one count—and the beauty of numbers of them. There is, of course, nothing new or unusual in the appeal of minerals. A silicate of aluminum and beryllium, two forms of alumina, isometric crystals of carbon, an alumino-fluoro-silicate, and various forms of silicon dioxide—i.e., emeralds, rubies and sapphires, diamonds, topazes, and amethysts, opals, and quartzes—among others have not only figured prominently in history but have caused a great deal of it, as have the metallic ores, upon which modern civilization has arisen.

It is not, however, the gemstones or other rare minerals or the exotic rocks that have the most to communicate. When you come to look into the history of the landforms around you, you find that what moves you most by the character you feel in them are the commonplace rocks, the yeoman rocks in which the earth's story is chiefly wrought. They comprise only a dozen or so basic types, and without requiring of you any special knowledge of chemistry they speak of elemental earth-processes and of an immeasurable past in which strange scenes with strange inhabitants (or none at all) have formed the landscapes of the earth and that which now is old was young. In them you feel you are close to the primal impulse and expression of creation. These are the rocks you are tempted to bring chunks of back with you from your travels—cobble-sized ones, at least, for rocks, if they are to be in character, must have heft. And if you do, you find that they may expand the horizons of the room where you install them to encompass the whole range of their places of origin, be it the tumbled boulders of Montauk Point, the crest of the Blue Ridge, or the Sierra Nevada.

Should mankind ever be moved to create of some august feature of the earth's surface a shrine to which men would repair expressly to think upon all that has gone into the forging of the lands they inhabit, there could well be set, to frame the entrance to the sanctuary, two shafts respectively of basalt and of granite. These are the rocks of which the earth's crust has been primarily fashioned.

Basalt, dense and heavy, ordinarily dark grey to nearly black, sometimes with a greenish cast to its dull hue, is the material of the earth's integument, underlying much of the oceans and continents. Granite is lighter—lighter in weight as well as in shade—but is still very hard. It is conspicuously granular (its name presumably coming from the Latin for "grain") and is distinguished by the pepper-and-salt effect of the black and glassy crystals it contains. In background color granite may be light to medium grey, salmon, rufous, or almost beef-color. For centuries it has been a favorite for every kind of monumental stonework; in fact, a visit to nearly any cemetery will give an idea of its range of hues. Hence, it is more generally familiar than basalt. Granite is predominantly the material of the continents. The continents vary in thickness but average about twenty-three miles from top to bottom. Where there are lowlands, the bottom is proportionately higher, and where there are mountain ranges, the bottom is deeper; in other words, the undersurface of a continent is roughly a reverse image of the upper. This has been shown both by gravitational measurements (granite exerts less attraction than the heavier rock below it) and by measurements of the speed of certain seismic waves that move faster through a denser than a lighter medium, just as sound waves move faster in water than

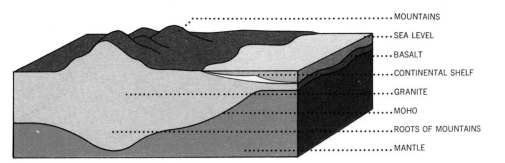

MOUNTAINS
SEA LEVEL
BASALT
CONTINENTAL SHELF
GRANITE
MOHO
ROOTS OF MOUNTAINS
MANTLE

in air. The highest mountains have roots extending as much as thirty miles down.

The continents have been likened to cakes of ice floating in water. Actually, the image would be more accurate if we imagine the surface of the water covered by a rubber blanket which the cakes of ice depress. The blanket is the layer of basalt.

Below the basaltic layer is the so-called mantle—an ill-chosen term since the portion of the earth it designates extends about halfway down to the earth's center. The spherical portion enveloped by the mantle, about two thousand miles in radius, is called the core. Interestingly enough, it would seem from the behavior of seismic waves that the material of the mantle, despite temperatures which would ordinarily be enough to melt it, is essentially solid because of the pressure it is under, while the material of the outer part of the core is so hot that despite the pressure it is under it is fluid, whereas the material of the inner core is, once again, despite its high temperature, under such pressure that it forms a solid. At the mantle's inner edge these pressures amount to one million times the pressure of the atmosphere at the surface, or one thousand tons to the square inch; at the center of the earth they are three times as great.

These figures, incidentally, give an idea of the fearsome power of gravity. Vaulting up a stairway two steps at a time—if we do—we may take this force lightly. We should be less likely to do so, however, if we could see an avalanche of snow thunder down a mountainside to wipe out a village, or feel the impact of a five-pound stone dropped on our foot. It is, presumably, radioactive material that keeps the earth hot within and may even be gradually warming it up. It is the sun's heat that evaporates water and forms the clouds, and the sun's heat in conjunction with the earth's spin that causes the winds and gives the earth its climate. But behind all geological change is the unremitting and inexhaustible power of gravity, as it is the power of gravity that holds the material of the earth in consolidation, the oceans in their beds, and the atmosphere bound to the earth. It is the power of gravity acting with greatest force on the densest material that keeps the continents afloat. It is gravity pulling without respite at every rock in the mountain's mass and drawing the scouring rains down from the heavens that gradually brings the mountains lower. And, whatever the mechanism by which mountains are raised again, we may say with confidence that without the power of gravity, acting as it does when it lifts a submarine to the surface, mountains would never be raised at all.

The material of the earth below the crust, presumably extending for hundreds of miles down and possibly constituting the entire mantle, is peridotite. This is a rock even harder and denser than basalt.

So far, peridotite is known to us only from the scattered outcrops where mountain-rearing forces have brought it unaltered to the surface. Ordinarily when it comes up from the depths it is transformed by the superheated aqueous fluids and vapors it encounters and emerges in resplendent guise befitting its status

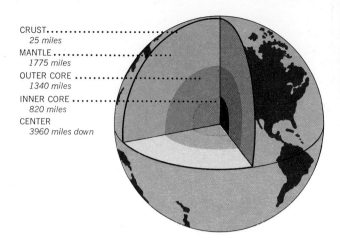

CRUST.........................
    25 miles
MANTLE....................
    1775 miles
OUTER CORE ....
    1340 miles
INNER CORE ....
    820 miles
CENTER
    3960 miles down

as lord of the underworld. It is known then as serpentinite, a rock formed mainly of the mineral serpentine. Smooth and waxy, bottle-green through blue-green, or green-blue to the black-green of a sea in the shadow of a cloud, as it is apt to be, serpentinite owes its color to serpentine, a mineral derived from olivine, one of the two magnesium-iron silicates of which peridotite is chiefly composed. That olivine, a mineral so beautiful that its most transparent crystals are mounted as gemstones, should be a leading component of our planet seems somehow against nature, yet such appears to be the case. (Olivine comes in varying shades of green and is known to jewelers as peridot or chrysolite.)

The boundary between the peridotitic mantle and the basaltic crust is a sharp one. It has been named the Mohorovičić discontinuity, after the Croatian seismologist who discovered it. For some years past, the American Academy of Sciences has had a plan to drill down into the "Moho," and in 1961 a hole almost six hundred feet deep was sunk in the ocean floor in 11,700 feet of water. (The ocean was chosen as a site in order to avoid having to drill through twenty-odd miles of continental rock, which would be four times as far as any hole has been drilled so far.) Drilling of the "Mohole" project began off the coast of California, but hopes of proceeding with the project in 1967 were dashed when Congress failed to appropriate funds for it.

Leaving out peridotite, which generally remains deep in the nether world, basalt and granite are the pre-eminent rocks of the class called igneous (of the same root as "ignite"), from which all other rocks are derived. Igneous rocks are those formed from molten rock. The viscous fluid, yellow-white with heat, with which they begin, originating deep inside the earth, is known as magma while it is underground and lava when and if it reaches the surface. (Why there have to be different names is unclear.) Rock that hardens deep underground is called plutonic; rock that hardens at or near the surface, volcanic. Plutonic rock is coarse-grained because the slow cooling of the magma gives the component elements time to sort themselves out and form into large mineral crystals. Correspondingly, volcanic rock is fine-grained, or even glassy if no time at all is allowed for the formation of crystals. Granitic rocks are mostly plutonic, volcanic rocks mostly basalt. In fact, when granitic rock is volcanic and fine-grained it is called not granite but rhyolite, while basaltic rock that is plutonic and coarse-grained is called gabbro, the name given it by Italian artisans.

The origin of granite is a matter of mystery and one vigorously debated. The assumption once was that with the hardening of the earth's crust continents of granite were left resting like slag on the denser material. (But no one knows that there were either continents or granite to begin with.) All that seems safe to say is that once a continent, always a continent. Once continents had been formed—however and wherever that might have been—it appears probable that they remained continents and, though at times partially flooded under shallow seas, never sank to become part of the ocean floor.

What militates against the granite-conti-

What is known of the earth's interior comes from indirect observation and deduction. The inner core is presumed to be solid; the outer core, liquid. The core comprises about 15 per cent of the earth's volume, the mantle about 84 per cent, and the crust the remaining 1 per cent. The boundaries between layers mark a change in material, though the exact composition of the layers beneath the crust can only be guessed at.

nents-as-original-slag theory is that no granite that might have been part of these original continents has yet been found. In fact, no granite has ever been found that had not, while fluid, intruded other, and necessarily older, rocks—basaltic lavas or rocks derived from pre-existing igneous rocks (which takes us a little ahead of our story). Contrary to what is widely believed, granite need not be an ancient rock, although, being formed as it is at great depths it is never exposed until uplift has taken place and thousands of feet of overlying rock have been worn away, which does not happen in less than many millions of years.

One possible explanation of the origin of granite rests upon the discovery that in a cooling basaltic magma the minerals that are the last to crystallize (chiefly silicon and potassium feldspar) are those that form granite, while the first to crystallize (the magnesium-iron silicates and calcium-sodium feldspar) are those that predominate in basalt. Thus granite could originate from the fluid drained or squeezed from such a partially crystallized basaltic magma. Moreover, basaltic magma might possibly derive in a similar way from peridotite. If so, it would seem to follow that the lavas erupted by volcanoes have been squeezed out of the peridotite of the mantle when it has become locally and partially liquefied. That at least might account for what otherwise remains totally mysterious.

This explanation of the creation of granite hardly goes far enough, however. Some other would seem to be needed for the giant granite batholiths (from the Greek words for "deep" and "rock") that take form at the core of great mountain ranges early in their genesis; it is such batholiths, surviving the ancient ranges, that make up so much of the continental basement. Certainly it is difficult to believe that these immense bodies, characteristically hundreds of miles long, were created by the "distillation" of a mere 10 per cent of the minerals in basalt.

What appears more likely is that the batholiths are constituted of the fused remains of earlier mountains that had started as granite and been through a series of transformations. Probably the whole truth is that the earth's store of granite is in permanent process of being reused and also of being added to by exudations of the mantle, and that the continents from perhaps very modest beginnings have tended to grow ever larger. But the question of how this could come about, which involves the question of how mountains come about, takes us back into mystery—though it is a mystery that, as we shall see, recent daring speculations may have resolved.

Whatever the origins of granite and of the granite batholiths, there seems to be no doubt that granite and other closely related rocks are the origin of most of the second-generation rocks, as they might be called. Constituted of the products of its disintegration, these form more than half the surface of the continents.

Only one thing can happen to exposed rock: attrition. Armed with fragments of the rock itself, flowing water proves in time an irresistible agent of destruction. Mere rivulets can sweep granules of rock with them and act as a file.

*Etched deep in the parched
landscape of California's Death
Valley, dried up stream
beds provide dramatic evidence of the power of erosion.
The braided pattern formed
by these gorge-like channels is
characteristic of desert areas,
where the surface material is
easily eroded, rainfall is light,
and streams carry sediments for
only a short distance, dumping
them in shallow, ephemeral
lakes instead of joining rivers
that connect with the sea.*

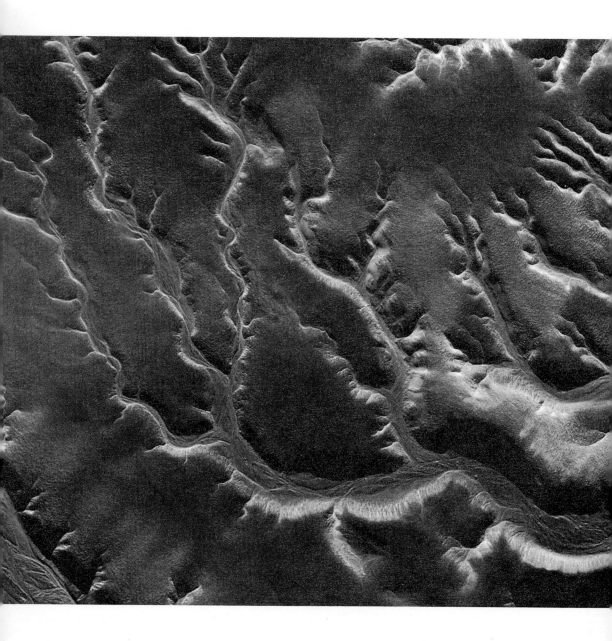

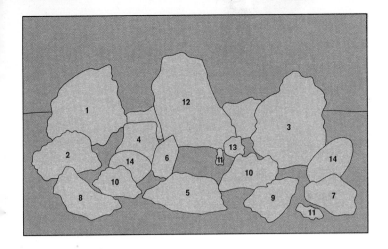

Plunging streams and rain-flooded mountain rivers can roll cobbles down their beds, adding hammer blows to the process of abrasion. Banks are undermined, cliffs collapse in rockfalls, arming the rushing waters with more weapons with which to batter and to grind. Even unflowing water wastes the rocks by producing chemical decomposition or by expanding as it freezes in rock crevices and thereby wedging pieces off. The lower slopes of most peaks are piled with slabs of rock called talus which have been dislodged in this way. Rock in a zone of nocturnal freezing and daily thawing suffers exceptional damage. In our climate, it is rock fragments pried loose by frost that supply mountain streams with most of their first teeth for grinding rock.

The remains of the split and crumbled rock are brought from higher elevations to lower, sometimes with long stopovers, but with the trend always downward. Rock, in effect, claims its own, for gravity is of course only the force of attraction exerted by the rock composing the planet. The fragments may be boulders that only the strongest currents can move. From these they range downward in size through pebbles and rock crumbs, which may be swept steadily along in a turbulent stream or lie at the bottom of brooks until snowmelt or downpours supply the flow to send them tumbling a few yards on, to silt so fine it will remain in suspension in the most gently roiled water. Ultimately the minerals may be reduced to molecules which remain indefinitely in solution, giving groundwater the taste that rainwater lacks and making the water of the oceans a vast treasury of chemicals.

The more thorough the going-over that the rock fragments are given, the more of them are reduced to the smaller-sized particles. In general, too, the finer the particles the farther they will be carried; as current slackens, it drops the heavier pieces first. A Dutch geologist, G. A. Neeb, computed that in an ocean current moving at a rate of an inch in 2.5 seconds a particle of fine sand will be carried about a mile while sinking a thousand yards; a particle of clay while sinking the same distance will be carried about eleven thousand miles. This is because the smaller an object the greater its surface in proportion to its weight—like a sailboat. Sand-sized grains are even transportable by winds of ordinary velocities, as is demonstrated by the formation of dunes wherever there is insufficient plant cover to tie down accumulations of such grains.

As long as the climate permits sufficient vegetation, large amounts of the detritus of the rocks will remain on the gentler slopes as soil, which is a mixture of rock remains and plant remains. For the rest, the spoils of the mountains are destined to end in a basin, and in general the greater the amount of water that is brought to bear and the longer time in which it is given to act, the larger will be the proportion that ends in that supreme basin, the ocean. One more generalization: the more opportunity water is given to work over the spoils, the more thoroughly it will sort them out and distribute them by size and weight and by mineral composition.

Granite disintegrates into quartz crystals,

which are hard and durable, and into crystals of feldspar, which deteriorate into clay and silica. The sands of our eastern beaches are composed mostly of quartz grains, though mixed with grains of feldspar. (The olive-hued beaches of Washington and Oregon have grains of basalt.) The clay and silt derived especially from the weathering of feldspar collect in mud flats in the backwaters of rivers and in the lagoons behind the outer beaches, but in the end the vast preponderance reaches the sea to be deposited at depths beyond the surf's reach.

Accumulating to thicknesses of thousands of feet along the coast and in shallower beds in lakes and interior bottomlands, the gravels, sands, and clays brought down by the streams are compacted by their own weight and through gradual cementation resolidified into sedimentary rock, as it is called. The chief bonding agents, deposited in the pores remaining after compaction, are calcium carbonate (also known as calcite or lime), silica, and iron oxide. Clay and silt are thus transformed into shale, sand into sandstone, and pebble-sized or larger sediments (usually with finer material filling the interstices) into rocks called conglomerates. Sandstones and shales are generally layered, the strata many feet thick or paper-thin. Ripple marks, animal tracks, and the fossilized skeletons of once-living creatures are frequently discovered in them when the rock is split between the strata. They are, indeed, the source of everything we know about the ancient seas.

Sedimentary rocks are characteristically somewhat soft or weak, but some sandstones are so resistant that when cracked the break will run through, not around, the grains of hard quartz. The walls of the original, central portion of the Capitol are made of a grey sandstone from the Potomac below Washington, similar to the walls of the White House (though these have been painted ever since it was necessary to hide the marks left when the British set fire to the mansion). The original Smithsonian building is of a reddish brown, local sandstone. The brownstone of the elegant old houses in New York is a similar sandstone. A conglomerate from a local quarry may be seen in the columns of Statuary Hall in the Capitol.

The husbandry of nature is not confined to the visible products of erosion. Dissolved minerals extracted from seawater by marine organisms and converted into protective coverings are destined to become rock. Reefs built by corals, algae, and worms may be hundreds of miles long. The valves of mollusks collect in deep beds. Casings secreted by protozoans called foraminifera filter to the bottom on the death of their inmates in a perpetual, imperceptible snow, to a depth of hundreds or thousands of feet. (The chalk cliffs of the English Channel are the edge of vast deposits of the casings.) All these are sources of limestone, a rock forming generally in shallow seas and, like sandstone and shale, by compaction and cementation. Jebel-al-Tarik—the Rock of Gibraltar—is a 1,400-foot limestone of mid-Mesozoic origin. The Dolomite Alps of Italy, rising to nearly eleven thousand feet, are composed of, and named after, a rock related to

limestone in which the calcium has been partly replaced by magnesium.

White in its pure form, limestone may be colored buff, brown, or reddish, like sandstone, by iron oxides, or grey or bluish by organic compounds. Being both firm and easily worked, it is a great favorite for ornamental building. The great pyramids of Egypt are of limestone. The Washington Monument in its lower section is of a coarse, crystalline marble, in its upper, of white dolomite, both from Maryland. The Pentagon and National Archives building are of Indiana limestone. Quite different in appearance, primarily because highly polished, is the creamy, variegated limestone forming the interior walls of the Smithsonian's Museum of History and Technology, in which, incidentally, may be observed intact pieces of coral and shell.

Silica is extracted from seawater by protozoans called radiolaria and by diatoms, algae that proliferate in the cooler waters of the ocean and form the base of the food-pyramid of the sea. Millions of square miles of the ocean's floor are covered by siliceous ooze consisting of the shells of these two single-celled organisms, as are many more millions of square miles covered by calcareous ooze consisting of the shells of foraminifera. (The balance, less than half, and most of it at great depths, is red clay.) Diatomite, which is used in industry for filters and insulation, is formed in the same way as limestone. While much less common in the earth's crust than limestone, it has been found in formations over half a mile in thickness, of which every cubic inch contains mil-

Since 1963, when it first exploded from the sea off Iceland's shore, the volcanic island Surtsey (below) has grown steadily and now exceeds a square mile in area. This very recent geologic drama, a windfall for scientific investigators, typifies the way the world's volcanic islands have been formed. On the right is a close-up of the volcano's fiery lava, also shown (below, right) in its cooled form along a slope.

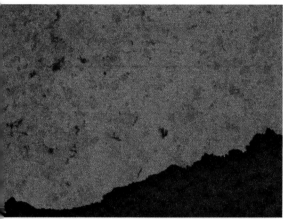

lions of diatom shells, each a marvel of design.

Although geologists do not exclaim over it, the process by which dissolved minerals are deposited molecule by molecule, to bond accumulations of free particles into solid rock, is surely a remarkable one. It must seem the more so, too, when we reflect that even desert sand dunes are converted into rock if stabilized by burial and percolated by water over a sufficiently long period. That there should be such a process seems quite fortuitous. The cementing agents have to go into solution in one set of widespread conditions and come out of it under another widespread but slightly different set; they must not, like table salt, be too soluble. Evidently, if the scales were tipped the least little bit one way or the other the earth would be an altogether different kind of place. Indeed, from what we are able to observe—although this may not be enough—we are justified in believing that without the cementation of sediments the erosion of the earth's rock would be irreversible and continuing. There might well be no land above water except for volcanic islands. Even given the transformation of loose sediments into rock, it does not follow that there should be land. Why does not such rock remain where it is formed, largely beneath the sea?

While making up only about 15 per cent of the outer ten miles of the earth's crust (according to computations by the Dutch geologist, Philip H. Kuenen), sedimentary rock, including limestone, covers three-quarters of the earth's land area. When metamorphosed sedimentary rock is included, the proportion is much higher. Sedimentary rocks are conspicuous in the formation of the greatest mountain ranges; fossils of marine animals have been found high up on the side of the world's loftiest mountain. All this cannot be explained by anything that is apparent about our planet and its processes.

There is more to be accounted for. No deposits from the deep sea—or for that matter from oceanic islands—older than the very late Mesozoic era have been found. Harry Hammond Hess, among others, has concluded that the average age of the ocean floor is only 100 to 200 million years and that "any sediment upon the sea floor ultimately gets incorporated in the continents." Far from being what we should expect from what is "evident," the processes that shape the earth are such that we must look speculatively deep into the interior of the planet, as geologists have done in the past few years, to come up with a hypothesis that, taking in all the known facts, would explain them.

Man has witnessed a continuing erosion of the earth's land area. It is not very surprising to anyone who has seen the Mississippi and the Colorado to learn that the two rivers between them carry a tenth of a cubic mile of sediments to the sea every year, although the Colorado is for the time being dumping its load behind man-made dams. By the same token, it is not hard to believe that the surface of the country as a whole is being lowered by one foot every nine thousand years by the thirty inches of rain that deluge it annually, at which rate it would be reduced to sea level in less than twenty-five million years. At the same time,

the only accessions to the land any human being has ever seen, apart from local accretions to the coast (which at best merely balance local subtractions), have been in the form of lava expelled from apertures in the earth's crust.

The human race is familiar enough with volcanoes. When Vesuvius, having given no signs of life in recorded times, erupted in A.D. 79 to bury Pompeii and Herculaneum in hot volcanic "ash"—actually flecks of rock—probably two thousand of the inhabitants perished through suffocation. Such explosions frequently precede the emission of lava by volcanoes. Another eruption after a long period of quiescence in 1631 is believed to have killed eighteen thousand. Over thirty thousand perished when Krakatoa, in the straits between Java and Sumatra, erupted in 1883 and about as many in the eruption of Mont Pelée on the West Indian island of Martinique in 1902.

What gives these volcanic eruptions their explosive force is the sudden vaporization of the water released from combination with magma. In the clouds of steam boiling up from an active crater we are probably witnessing the origins of the oceans. Water, the enemy of rock, is probably born of rock.

Some of the most productive volcanoes—if that is the term—are comparatively non-explosive. The fire-fountains that periodically rise from Mauna Loa in Hawaii, for example, are only curtain-raisers, in a literal sense, to the full-scale eruption, in which highly fluid lava simply wells up out of the crater and from the many fissures radiating from it to pour like a fiery soup down the slopes. Built up by many

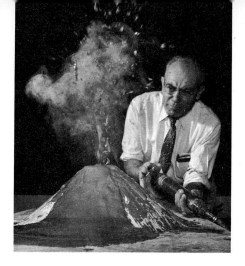

layers of such free-flowing lava, Mauna Loa and its sister volcanoes have gentle slopes and low profiles. They belong to a class known as shield volcanoes—in contrast to so-called composite volcanoes, of which Fujiyama is the archetype, which are built up of alternative layers of extruded lava and exploded ash and rock and form steep-sided cones. Yet so enormous are the outpourings of lava that have created the Hawaiian Islands that the highest summits stand almost thirty thousand feet above the Pacific's floor, more than thirteen thousand feet above the water.

Upwellings of lava are not everywhere as localized as they are in single volcanoes. In Iceland, one of the most volcanic of all regions, lava poured for two years beginning in 1783 from a rent fifteen miles long, creating a dust cloud that hung over Europe and part of North America and produced the "year without a summer." As against 218 square miles covered by basalt in the 1783 eruption in Iceland, fissure eruptions in prehistoric times have buried areas of more than one hundred thousand square miles to depths of over a mile, though probably over millions of years.

While men have often enough, and generally to their sorrow, witnessed this most theatrical of geological processes, the causes of volcanism remain conjectural. How does the mass of molten rock expelled from within the earth come into being? The once prevalent notion that the earth is a molten sphere with a thin outer crust, which, when ruptured, permits the escape of some of the fluid material within, has had to be abandoned. The behavior of seismic

waves shows that the ill-named mantle (the zone between the crust and the core) has the character of a solid, despite its high temperature, clearly because of the pressure it is under. Perhaps the most widely held theory is that the material of the mantle becomes locally liquefied when the pressure is relaxed. The best clue as to why and how this comes about would seem to be offered by the distribution of volcanoes, which obviously is not random or haphazard. Most volcanoes are located in a belt through the Mediterranean area, along the Mid-Atlantic Ridge (which lies, significantly enough, as we shall see, just about midway between the opposite shores of the Atlantic) and around the rim of the Pacific in the "ring of fire." The pattern approximates that in which most earthquakes occur. And it also follows roughly the zones in which mountain-raising forces seem to be most active.

No one has ever, at least knowingly, seen a mountain grow by so much as a cubit, except through volcanic action. (Parícutin, starting as a hole in a Mexican farmer's field in 1943, in ten years grew to a cinder cone twelve hundred feet high.) All that is known of the process by which rock formed beneath the sea is elevated to create new land has come through inference. That human beings, who, no longer ago than it takes granite to weather a few inches, were displaying the height of their mental powers in affixing a stone to the end of a stick, have been able to reconstruct the process of mountain-building as well as they have through reading the rocks is surely almost as remarkable as the process itself.

THE EARLY INSIGHTS

In the literature and art of the Renaissance we find human beings represented very much as we know them; it is not easy to find fault with Shakespeare's grasp of character or Michelangelo's of human form. By contrast, the picture of the physical universe entertained four or five centuries ago is at violent odds with reality. The earth sciences, among others, are very young. They might, however, have been much farther along in the past than they were had not the great beginning that was Greece been aborted by internecine conflict and foreign invasion.

The Greeks brought to the world the novelty of looking at all things with interested and open eyes and drawing reasoned conclusions. By the sixth century B.C. two Greeks, Thales of Miletus and Xenophanes of Colophon, had made two of the crucial discoveries of geology: the one that the sea can both wear away the land and build it up, the other that fossils of fish and shells prove that the sea once covered dry land. ("From earth all things are, and to earth all things return," Xenophanes declared.) To these the Greek geographer Strabo, in the first century B.C., added the refinement that the same lands, even continents, are sometimes elevated above the sea and at others depressed beneath it. Meanwhile, in about 250 B.C., Aristarchus of Samos had proposed that the earth moved around the sun and Eratosthenes of Alexandria had calculated the circumference of the planet with extraordinary accuracy.

Some fifteen centuries were to elapse before Western civilization would begin recovering the ground that was lost after the decline of Greece. It was not until 1543, with the publication of Copernicus' great work, that the earth was once more seen to revolve around the sun. Leonardo da Vinci, who knew that the earth was round, had meanwhile announced that the fossils found in rocks, of which he had turned up many in his work as an engineer, were remains of once-living things that had been buried in the mud when the land was beneath the sea. He also described the role of precipitation in shaping the topography.

That was a good beginning, and Leonardo was not the only exemplar of a new, inquiring, rational spirit. Francis Bacon spoke for many when he said, "Man, the servant and interpreter of nature, can do and understand so much, and so much only, as he has observed in fact or in thought of the course of nature," and, "All depends on keeping the eye steadily fixed upon the facts of nature, and so receiving their images simply as they are; for God forbid that we should give out a dream of our own imagination for a pattern of the world."

Such a spirit was, however, certain to run head-on into entrenched theology, and it did. Men whose position depended on the unassailable authority of the church and hopes of eternal life on the absolute factual reliability of the Bible were implacable antagonists of the essential testimony of the rocks. Fossils were explained as everything but what they were—as the creation of vapors within rocks, as models with which the Creator had practiced, as the Devil's handiwork designed to try men's faith—for fossils were crucial. If they were

what they were, the earth was not created in six days or in the year 4004 B.C., as Archbishop James Ussher in 1655 calculated it was. And Biblical chronology did not allow a great deal of latitude either way. Moreover, the Flood was central to Christian thinking about the distant past. Its hold was so strong that even many geologists, a number of whom were theologians who had been drawn into "natural philosophy," long sought to reconcile their findings with a catastrophic, global inundation. As late as 1829 a leading American in the field, Professor Benjamin Silliman of Yale, protested that "Regarding the deluge, there can be but one opinion. . . . Geology fully confirms the scripture history of that event." The prevalence of sedimentary rock might have seemed to argue in favor of a great flood, and there were many to say it did. What was left unexplained was how the turbulent waters ("inconceivably violent torrents and cataracts everywhere descending the hills and mountains and meeting a tide rising at the rate of more than seven hundred feet in twenty-four hours," as Silliman reckoned must have been the case) could have laid down such precisely organized and sharply distinguished silts, sands, and gravels. To consider such questions openly remained a dangerous activity until well along in the nineteenth century.

For two and a half centuries after Leonardo the steps by which geology was advanced were limited and generally resisted or ignored. In 1669, eight years after the term "geology" was coined, the Danish naturalist Nicolaus Steno proposed that rock strata had been and were

still being precipitated from fluids and were all originally horizontal. Jean Etienne Guettard, a French botanist and physician, went much further and propounded the unheard-of doctrine that strata were not haphazard but extended across the country in a recognizable order; those around Paris he represented in two maps published in 1752.

The discoverer of an assemblage of extinct volcanoes in the Auvergne, Guettard was followed by Nicolas Desmarest, an inspector-general of French manufactures, who in 1763 recognized that the prismatic basalt in the Auvergne was a form of lava. That important discovery was matched by another. The changes Desmarest found in the succession of volcanic rocks wrought by erosion led him to realize that valleys originate from the action of streams and are not clefts dramatically and mysteriously opened up on the earth's surface of which streams have merely taken advantage. This truth would seem self-evident to us today, for nothing is as obvious as that which has been made so by the exertions of one's predecessors. Yet the general validity of Desmarest's conclusion was not established until 1869 when John Wesley Powell made his daring descent of the Colorado River.

Perhaps more important than any discovery by Guettard or Desmarest was their demonstration of the value of getting out and seeing, for both were great rovers. Had their example been heeded by the geognostic—as he would have called himself—who was to be more in the public eye than anyone else in his field in the years that immediately followed, geology

might have been put forward by a decade or two. Of Abraham Gottlob Werner, who taught mineralogy at Freiberg for forty years beginning in 1775, it has been said: "That timid little man was perhaps the greatest teacher that has ever faced a laboratory class. . . . The greatest, perhaps, but certainly among the most mistaken."

Werner brought system to the study of minerals and not only showed that the subject was intellectually worthy of respect, but aroused enthusiasm for it as well. He also showed that rock strata lay upon one another in a definite sequence. Unfortunately, he took as his premise that the sequence in which they occurred around Freiberg was that in which they also occurred everywhere else in the world. On top of that, he decreed that all rocks were precipitates of a former universal ocean and were deposited in four stages, each of which was everywhere laid down at the same time. As many had before him and have since, he made up in positiveness for what he lacked in evidence; and not for the first time a dogma that explained everything in terms of a few simple conceptions, reiterated with undeviating conviction, found ready disciples. Freiberg became an international center of "geognosy"—earth knowledge—and on both sides of the ocean Werner's teaching was to distort the thinking of the susceptible for half a century to come.

But *Wernerismus* was doomed from that day in 1785 when James Hutton, a 59-year-old Scotsman—a chemist turned progressive farmer turned explorer of rocks—in the hills north of Edinburgh found a dike of red granite cutting through strata of limestone and schist. (Hutton's excitement was such that his guide thought he had discovered gold.) Unmistakably, the granite in a molten state had invaded pre-existing rocks which Werner had assigned to a later age and had baked them along the planes of contact. Granite was neither a precipitate nor necessarily aboriginal, as Werner had insisted. In that same year Hutton presented a paper to the Royal Society of Edinburgh which may be said to have marked the birth of the science of geology.

In his two-volume *Theory of the Earth* published in 1795, Hutton went a long way toward presenting a picture of the geological processes as we know them today, showing that the rocks of the earth's surface were in large part composed of the detritus of older rocks which had accumulated and been compacted beneath the seas, tilted and upreared to form new mountains (in which process molten rock was forced into cracks of existing rocks), and that these new mountains were in turn destined to wear away and the cycle to be repeated. What Hutton taught was revolutionary in its breathtaking comprehensiveness. It was no less so in the view he urged that the forces that produced the earth as we know it were precisely those that we see around us today.

The principle of uniformitarianism, as it came to be called, cut directly across the prevailing conviction that the earth had been given its form and prepared for man's occupancy by sudden interventions of convulsive, shattering force, and in comparatively recent years at that. Those brought up on the Old Testament vision of Creation must have felt a chill touch their hearts at the suggestion that the earth they inhabited owed its features only to automatic and generally undramatic and imperceptible processes and that these processes, as Hutton saw them, had "no vestige of a beginning, no prospect of an end."

The wider the vistas science has opened up the further has man been demoted from the position he once held at the center of the cosmos as its preordained beneficiary and reason for being. To the shock thus administered, geology has made its full contribution. If it has not, like astronomy, revealed the unthinkable immensity of space, it has brought home to us the no less unthinkable boundlessness of time. It has, moreover, done its share in destroying the belief that we inhabit a world of finished products, permanent in character.

The anguish and anger with which the implications of science have been resisted are easy to understand. And yet, as deeply unsettling as they have been, the panoramas that have been disclosed are surely exhilarating and exalting, like the views from a mountaintop in which visible creation gains in sublimity from a vantage point in which man's place is diminished. Beyond that there are consolations in the knowledge that all is process. The corollary is—and this, too, science has shown—that there are no differences in kind but only differences in degree. Through the spectrum from the redwood down through one-celled plants and animals up to man there is perfect and complete gradation, and it is only because so many of the links have perished or are invis-

At left, standing face to face with several peculiar-looking rock formations is eighteenth-century geologist James Hutton, who attacked the naive, dogmatic, but influential ideas of Abraham Werner and put geology on a firm scientific footing. Werner had described the history of the earth as a series of discrete periods, each with a particular kind of geologic activity; Hutton recognized that the earth's past was vastly more complicated.

ible that we are generally unmindful of this truth. If no form of life had ever become extinct, it is quite possible that all living things would have to be grouped in a single species for lack of any break in the progression from one kind to another. Similarly, it becomes increasingly evident that between living and non-living things there is no clear division. Are viruses alive or do they merely act as if they were? The distinction is perhaps merely semantic. There is unity in the universe of a completeness unsuspected by our ancestors, and of this unity we are a part. Between us and that pink gneiss, 3.6 billion years old, there is unbroken intergradation and continuity. Like Kipling's Mowgli addressing the snake people, we can declare to all things, and with a more informed conviction than is likely to have been his: "We be of one blood, thou and I."

Such a view was far in the future, however, when Hutton died in 1797. Catastrophism and Wernerism still gripped men's minds, and Hutton's formulations, couched as they were in ponderous and difficult English, fell into disregard. It remained for Charles Lyell, born the year of Hutton's death, to revive them and carry them forward.

Meanwhile a man had appeared on the scene, walking hundreds of miles with transit and notebook, carried over country roads in jolting coaches, who was to give geology the kind of grounding it most required at this stage. Born in 1769 and brought up by an Oxfordshire farmer, William Smith showed his bent in boyhood by collecting "pundibs" and "pound-stones," which probably few of his neighbors recognized as the relics of once-living organisms. He went on to become, as the Geological Society declared in honoring him many years later, "the first, in this country, to discover and to teach the identification of strata, and to determine their succession, by means of their imbedded fossils." As a surveyor for a canal, later as a consulting engineer, he covered England, observing the strata and correlating them in accordance with the types of plants and animals that inhabited the shores and sea bottoms on which they were initially laid down as sediments. Smith perceived that "the same strata were found always in the same order and contained the same fossils" and recognized, as no one had before, that strata containing the same fossils must be the same age, no matter where found or what their composition. A procrastinator at desk work who was continually afield, Smith left it uncertain for years what fruit his labors would bear. Only the pressure of friends and financial needs, together with the danger that others, making use of the information he had given out piecemeal, would gain the credit for the work he had done, prodded him into action. The result, when it came in 1822, was a wholly unprecedented *Geological Atlas of England and Wales*, consisting of twenty-one county maps in color that gave geology new organization, utility, and authority.

Charles Lyell, of a landed family of Scotland, was, like his friend Charles Darwin, an amateur in science in an age when science without amateurs would have been hard put to it indeed. His great work was his *Principles of*

Geology, to which he devoted most of his life. The first edition came out in 1830 when Lyell was only thirty-three, but he was busy revising the twelfth when he died in 1875. Each successive edition of this renowned work, it has been said, was "so enriched with new material and the results of riper thoughts as to form a complete history of the progress of geology during that interval."

Charles Lyell was a gentleman and far from self-assertive; because of a speech impediment public appearances were difficult for him. Yet he threw down the gage plainly enough in the subtitle of his *Principles:* "An Attempt to Explain the Former Changes in the Earth's Surface by Reference to Causes Now in Operation." It was still possible in 1836 for the author of a geological survey of Nova Scotia to refer to "that overwhelming deluge" as having probably been preceded by "the depression of whole continents, the raising of the ocean's level bed, the distortion of strata previously horizontal, the elevation of mountains, and all those violent operations whereby the whole surface of this planet has been rent asunder." But the pressure of Lyell's evidence and Lyell's reasoning was irresistible. "The great merit of the *Principles,*" said Darwin, "was that it altered the whole tone of one's mind. . . ." Before Charles Lyell had finished, catastrophism was ancient history; the patient amassing and analysis of facts was established as the method of geology and the science was much as we know it today.

Lyell made two trips to the United States, the first in 1841. Traveling about the East, he met many geologists and undoubtedly contributed greatly to the state of the science in the New World.

There was room for such a contribution. Geology did not lack for practitioners in the new nation. This was the era of state surveys designed to explore the possibilities of profitable mining and produce information of use to agriculture. But geological processes were not well understood and data not always easy to come by. Distances were great, forest covered much of the country, and the opportunities to see below the surface were so scanty that the reports even of well-diggers assumed a prime importance.

"He went forth with his hammer in hand and his wallet on his shoulder, pursuing his researches in every direction, often amid pathless tracts and dreary solitudes, until he had crossed and recrossed the Allegheny mountains no less than fifty times. He encountered all the privations of hunger, thirst, fatigue, and exposure, month after month and year after year, until his indomitable spirit had conquered every difficulty and crowned his enterprise with success."

This passage from a contemporary biography of William Maclure, while surely overdrawn and exaggerated, says a good deal about the trials of the early geologists. Maclure himself, a Scotsman who came to the United States in 1796 and was for twenty years president of the Philadelphia Academy of Natural Sciences, has been called the Father of American Geology on the strength of his *Observations on the Geology of the United States*, published in 1809.

This included a map of the country east of the Mississippi, most parts of which the author had visited, showing in six colors the distribution of the main categories of rocks as he understood it. Possibly the most remarkable thing about Maclure's work was that one of such scope could be produced at all at that time and that, meager and often misconstrued as his information was, his map bears as much resemblance as it does to those of a century and a half later.

"A heterogeneous thing," Amos Eaton called Maclure's book eleven years later, then added: "but I can find a better application to facts in his book than in all American works." This was perhaps faint praise since in the very same letter Eaton declared, "I have now ascertained, to my full satisfaction, that I am the only person in North America capable of judging rock strata." There may have been one less competent person than Eaton allowed if we may judge by his report of petrified roots of mountain laurel in sandstone a hundred million years older than the oldest flowering plants of any kind. Eaton, moreover, had no trouble accounting for the upheaval of mountains by the combustion of unidentified inflammables deep in the earth at their foreordained sites. Still, it was to be a long time before anyone thought of a better device than heat for lifting the mountains.

Amos Eaton may have been an opinionated theorizer, but he won respect for his calling by his devotion to it as a lecturer, put technical education in the United States far ahead of where he found it by creating Rensselaer In-

stitute and, indefatigable in application, was one of those through whom the anatomy of the continent was being gradually delineated. His most ambitious work was a geological survey of the area of the Erie Canal, undertaken in 1824. This included a cross section from Lake Erie to Boston, the eastern part of which was contributed by Edward Hitchcock.

A native of Deerfield, Massachusetts, Hitchcock was a Congregational minister who became the leading geologist of New England, the architect of the first complete state geological survey (that of Massachusetts, of 1830-33), and president of Amherst College. He thus, it might be said, lived up to the promise he showed at the age of eighteen, when, responding to the offer by the publisher of an almanac to pay ten dollars on the discovery of an error in its tables, he pointed out a sheaf of them in the astronomical section, then, repaid only by the publisher's slighting retort, disclosed twenty in the figures used for navigation and an additional thirty-five in the next edition.

Hitchcock was not one to be hustled out of the ways of the past. Because it crossed a high "greenstone ridge," he was unable to believe that the Connecticut River could have excavated its channel on its own—as it had—and, a catastrophist opposed to Lyell, he insisted that volcanic forces far greater than any today were required to upheave the continents from the ocean bottom and the mountains from the lowlands. But in his voluminous scientific writings he was a pioneer too. In his reflections, for example, on a strangely transformed conglomerate from Newport, Rhode Island, containing

During the nineteenth century geology came of age and interest in it became widespread among writers, artists, and intellectuals who, increasingly, found in science a new vision of nature against which to relate their own vision of man. At right, in an 1849 painting by Asher Durand, poet William Cullen Bryant and artist Thomas Cole, both noted science enthusiasts, stand amidst a panorama of geologic history in the Catskills.

elongated and flattened pebbles, he took a long step toward an understanding of metamorphism; and, studying the folded strata of the Vermont hills, he was the first to realize that lateral as well as vertical forces were involved in mountain-making.

That a man of Hitchcock's position—and he was the first president of the American Association for the Advancement of Science—should have spent the last years of a distinguished career endeavoring to reconcile science with "the Hebrew poem of the creation as substantial history" (in the words of a memorialist) gives an idea of the atmosphere in which geology had to grow up. The creation at Yale in 1802 of a professorship of chemistry and natural science was not only unprecedented but daring. However, the requirements of the chair were such that they could be met by a 22-year-old tutor at law, Benjamin Silliman, who, from knowing nothing at all about the subjects he was to teach, qualified himself by attending lectures for five months at the Medical School of Philadelphia—and that only after satisfying himself that "occasionally reading . . . privately" from "a few books on chemistry" would not suffice. If Silliman seems a peculiar choice for the job he was to perform, at least he was a safe one. And perhaps that is the point. As Thomas Huxley later put it, he wrote "with one eye on fact and the other on Genesis." Yet by the time Silliman died, in the same year as Hitchcock (1864), he had, in the view of George P. Merrill, a leading historian of American geology, "done more to advance the science of geology than any other man of his day.

The great contribution of men like Silliman and Eaton was that they prepared the way for the emergence of a different sort: the truly professional scientists. The change could perhaps be marked by the debut of a young man who had walked back and forth between his home in Hingham and Boston, where Professor Silliman was lecturing, and who had gone on to Rensselaer to become a student, protégé, and, in turn, inspirer of Amos Eaton. James Hall may be said to mark the beginning of the modern age of geology in the United States in another sense as well. Though born in 1811, he could well be remembered by persons now alive, for he lived until 1898, active to the last, having made a trip to the Ural Mountains of Russia in his eighty-sixth year.

"Take him all in all, Professor Hall was a great man," a fellow geologist wrote of him the year after he died. "His excellences were towering, his faults glaring. . . . His friends would do anything for him; his enemies would do anything against him." Though most of his work was in geology, his *magnum opus* was a paleontology of New York filling seventeen quarto volumes, the major portion of which was financed by appropriations Hall wrested year after year from the state legislature by sheer, relentless force of personality.

It was with Hall that geology took the first, sure stride to an understanding of the origin of folded-mountain belts, which is perhaps central to an understanding of the evolution of the earth. And the mountains in which Hall made his crucial discoveries were, as might have been expected, the Appalachians.

Time is the great equalizer, the great modifier of terrain, the leveler, the softener of features—and the East is old. Easterners are given little reason to be conscious of the dynamism of the earth or to think of it with awe. Their landscape is for the most part rural or pastoral. Nature in the East is flora and fauna, and relatively tame ones; it is hardly the earth at all. In the East, the drama of the natural scene inheres in winds, clouds that scud across the moon or build snowy masses to domes high in the summer sky, thunderstorms and blizzards, and the change of seasons. There is, of course, the shore—Easterners gravitate to it. But here the protagonist is the sea, the sea that is the ancient adversary of the land. On the East Coast the shore is only a passive defendant and, south of New England, a depressed one on a frontier periodically assaulted by storms and hurricanes.

But there is an exception. There are the Appalachian Mountains. It is an unprivileged Easterner indeed who has not known the sight of their ranges rising ahead of him like the waves of a tumultuous ocean; the closing in of the forested slopes of the foothills; the lift of the heart as the land falls away below; the air turning clean and cool as spring water, fragrant with the forest; the feeling of having entered a higher realm of timeless tranquillity; and above all, the massive presence of the great humped ridges themselves and the sense they convey—that the ultimate voice is after all not man's.

It is fair to assume an indulgent smile on the part of Westerners when Easterners make

something of their age-worn hills. The highest summits of the Appalachians stand no higher than the valleys of the Rocky Mountains. Yet if the Appalachians are to be slighted on that account, one who has stood on the threshold of the still-growing Himalayas and beheld the pinnacle of Nanga Parbat towering to its terrifying height in the heavens might take a deprecating view of Pikes Peak, which rises to an altitude little more than half as great. But these things are relative, and even if they were not, the fact is that the loftiest of the Appalachians stand about as high above their valleys as the Rocky Mountains do, which is to say a mile or more. Even to one newly arrived from Colorado, the spectacle of New Hampshire's Presidential Range can seem as momentous as that of the Front Range of the Rockies.

The North Carolina ranges are even higher, and they stretch away for seventy-five miles from east to west. When you gaze across them in the evening from a point of vantage, at the hour when dusk fills the coves, they look like a wilderness even today. You can understand the menace they held for the early settlers and can appreciate how the Appalachians' complex system of heavily forested, precipitous ridges, choked with tangle along the watercourses and natural passes, could have dammed the westward tide of empire for a hundred years— about as long as it took the tide to cross the rest of the continent once the Appalachians were breached.

The spruce and balsam forests of the northland are here sprinkled over the mountains above five thousand feet, solidly mantling many of the summits; they give the Green Mountains their name. Quitting the coast in central Maine, these forests, as you progress southward, pull back to even higher elevations. By driving twenty miles or so in the southern Appalachians you may thus accomplish the equivalent of a thousand miles of horizontal travel up the coast, for temperature drops about a degree for every two hundred feet of altitude gained.

The length of the Appalachian chain as conventionally conceived is fifteen hundred miles or a little more—again, not very impressive compared with the Rocky Mountain chain, which is six thousand miles long, if you count the Aleutians and its extension into Central America. But there is good reason to believe that the conventional conception of the Appalachians is very inadequate.

In the north the system reaches its climax in the White Mountains. The Presidential Range rises to timber line and beyond, though it does so not so much by virtue of the elevation of its domed and gently peaked summits as because no trees could withstand the savagery of the winter gales that lash them. These have exceeded two hundred miles an hour—the highest ever recorded on earth—on Mount Washington, which rises to 6,288 feet, a rocky, arctic island, it has been called, on a pedestal above New England. Snow falls every month of the year on Mount Washington, and since a New Hampshire settler named Darby Field and some Indian guides first climbed it in 1642 a number of lives have been lost there through failure to reckon on unseasonable blasts.

Westward across the Connecticut River, the Green Mountains of Vermont are less formidable; their highest, Mount Mansfield, is under 4,400 feet. Farther on, the Adirondacks rise to elevations a thousand feet higher than the Green Mountains and dominate Lake Champlain, which divides the two ranges. Whatever the form of mountains to begin with, the forces of weathering tend to carve them into likenesses of one another, and the Adirondacks resemble the major parts of the Appalachians. But the two systems have quite different origins and were brought into being by different processes.

From the Green Mountains a branch of the Appalachians runs north to form the Notre Dame Mountains and the Shickshocks of the Gaspé Peninsula; here, reaching a height of over four thousand feet, the system forms the southern bank of the wide cleft occupied by the St. Lawrence and for the first time meets the ocean. Another branch extends from the White Mountains through western Maine and on into New Brunswick, south of the Gaspé. It achieves its supreme elevation in northern Maine in the scimitar ridge of Mount Katahdin, a mile-high monadnock, as geologists call a solitary mountain (from Mount Monadnock in southwestern New Hampshire), which of all parts of our country first catches the morning sun. A third branch, southeast of the other two, forms the low backbone of Nova Scotia. All three on reaching the Gulf of St. Lawrence dip beneath the water. But even this is not the finish. The Appalachians re-emerge in the northeast-trending highlands of Newfoundland, chief among which is Long Ridge, with heights of more than two thousand feet. The end comes at last in the bleak and forbidding cliffs, several hundred feet in height, with which Newfoundland fronts the North Atlantic.

Or does it? Off the coast of Newfoundland the Labrador current passes inland of the Gulf Stream and the proximity of the cold water and the warm produces the fogs so well known to the boatmen of the Grand Banks. From the brink of the continent we look into mists both literal and figurative. It is uncharacteristic of mountains of the type of the Appalachians to terminate so abruptly, and . . . and across the Atlantic there are other ranges of similar rocks equally weathered that rise from the sea: the Caledonian Mountains of Northern Ireland, Wales, and Scotland, which were formed in mid-Paleozoic times (like a forerunner of the Appalachians which arose on what is now the western side of the range's curved northern portion) and the mountains of southern Ireland, Cornwall, and Brittany, which (like the Appalachians) were formed in late Paleozoic times. Were the ranges, now divided by the Atlantic, once joined? The question, as we shall see, arises again in connection with the mystery of the origin of the sediments that went into the making of the Appalachians.

From the upper New England highlands the Appalachians taper off southward through the Berkshires of western Massachusetts and Connecticut—a prolongation of the Green Mountains—and are severed by the Hudson River. One would not ordinarily speak of mountains as severed by a river, but the Hudson is more

Petulant, cantankerous, and dictatorial, the geologist James Hall nonetheless greatly advanced and influenced American geologic thought. His concept that a deep basin of depression always precedes mountain-making is still standard in modern geology. He also founded American stratigraphy and pioneered in invertebrate paleontology, and he served as state geologist for Iowa, Wisconsin, and New York.

than that; it is an arm of the sea, a fiord, tidal for 150 miles inland. (Henry Hudson, in 1609, may be forgiven for believing it a passage to the Pacific.) The Hudson and its tributary the Mohawk constitute the one significant break in the Appalachian chain south of the St. Lawrence. At one time the Great Lakes drained through them to the sea, and the immense volume of water the Hudson carried then may have had something to do with the extraordinary, deep canyon it has cut from its present mouth across the continental shelf—the submerged margin of the continent, some 125 miles wide off New York—down the continental slope and even out across the ocean's floor for another one hundred miles or so, at depths of up to two miles.

Below the Hudson River, the characteristic anatomy of the southern Appalachians soon asserts itself. Beginning modestly as a long ridge known in Pennsylvania and Maryland as South Mountain (where the Army of Northern Virginia delayed the Army of the Potomac for a vital day before the Battle of Antietam), the press of steep and rugged mountains called the Blue Ridge, which makes up the eastern province of the southern Appalachians, quickly reaches four thousand feet in northern Virginia and gains in breadth and elevation through North Carolina before it runs out in Georgia.

More often than not, the term "Blue Ridge" is restricted to the belt of mountains on the extreme east, which overlook the low hills of the Piedmont. Of these the highest is Grandfather Mountain, just south of Blowing Rock, North Carolina. While it does not quite reach six

thousand feet, this stalwart, which stands out from forty miles away, must be one of the most imposing of the Appalachians. Actually, however, all the ranges east of the Great Smokies would appear to be one family, geologically; all have cores of ancient, Precambrian rock. It would seem more reasonable to consider them all as embraced in the Blue Ridge, including the Black Mountains, north of Asheville, which rise to 6,684 feet in Mount Mitchell—the highest elevation in the eastern half of the country.

The Great Smokies, straddling the border of North Carolina and Tennessee, are of less ancient and less worked-over but still Precambrian rock. They are the Appalachians *par excellence*, a wilderness of lordly eminences, sixteen of them over six thousand feet in height —Clingmans Dome, the highest, being only forty feet lower than Mount Mitchell—characteristically overhung with mists and shrouded in a magnificent forest richer in species than perhaps any other of its extent in the world's temperate regions, all mercifully preserved in a National Park of over 760 square miles.

On the other side of the Smokies and the Blue Ridge, looking inland, is the Great Valley, the most famous sector of which is the Shenandoah Valley of Virginia. South of the Shenandoah, the long trough incorporates the upper Tennessee Valley and finally debouches onto the coastal plain at Birmingham, Alabama. In the other direction, after becoming the Cumberland Valley in Maryland, it runs northeastward to encompass Harrisburg and Allentown in Pennsylvania, passes beneath

Kittatinny Ridge just inside the extreme northwestern border of New Jersey, and reaches the Hudson River between Newburgh and Kingston.

Westward of the Great Valley are ranges of fossil-bearing, sedimentary rock, younger than and very different from the forged rock of the Blue Ridge Mountains and of the major New England ranges. They extend from Alabama on up through Pennsylvania and New Jersey, thence as the Taconic Range along the border between New York and the New England states and into Quebec, forming the Notre Dame and Shickshock mountains of the Gaspé Peninsula. In their mid-section especially, from Tennessee through Pennsylvania, they consist of long, level ridges roughly parallel with one another and with the trend of the Appalachians as a whole.

Still farther to the west come the Appalachian Plateaus—the Allegheny Plateau from the Mohawk and Hudson rivers south through West Virginia, the Cumberland Plateau from Kentucky southward into Alabama. The former overlooks the parallel ridges to the east in the dramatic escarpment called the Allegheny Front. In the Catskills its peaks top four thousand feet, while West Virginia's Spruce Knob is 4,860 feet. Even as far south as this the Allegheny Plateau reaches up into the climatic zone of the northern forest, and enthusiasts drive 150 miles from the nation's capital to West Virginia's high, cool bogs to hear the hermit thrush sing at its southernmost breeding station. More to the point, in the view of many, the Appalachian Plateaus mean coal—

coal beds from one end almost to the other, and near the two ends, iron, as witness Pittsburgh and Birmingham. Less happily, they mean mountainsides ravaged by strip-mining, barren hills of spoils, a history of destructive lumbering, backwoods farms of thin, infertile, eroded soils, and poverty: Appalachia.

Not having been uplifted as mountains, the plateaus, in the language of geology, are mountainous only "topographically," as the result of erosion. Yet they are that, surely, and in as patternless a way as the waves thrown up in a tide rip. But for the natural corridors of which the Wilderness Road from Cumberland Gap (where Virginia, Tennessee, and Kentucky come together) and the Cumberland Road from Cumberland, Maryland, took advantage, the plateaus would have imposed an even more redoubtable barrier to migration westward than they did.

The rock strata of which the plateaus and adjacent ranges are formed gave rise to perhaps the first important American contribution to geological theory. It was James Hall who was the originator.

The start came in 1836 when Hall was one of four men appointed to do a geological survey of New York. As the youngest, Hall was assigned the western part of the state, considered of least interest. Those who predicted slim pickings had, however, not reckoned on Hall's character, in which, we are told, there was "a childlike simplicity united to self-confidence and indomitable energy." Hall found in his territory a succession of early Paleozoic strata abounding in fossils and exposed in a most orderly fashion from Lake Ontario southward like courses of shingles, but shingles on a roof with a reverse slope: Ordovician, Silurian, Devonian. . . . Hall not only "solved" the geology of western New York but provided the key to the more complicated formations to the east and to the structure of the interior lowlands as a whole. He also discovered that the strata in the Appalachians, while identical to those on the west, were much deeper. Each stratum appeared to be wedge-shaped, tapering off to the west, enormously thickening to the heart of the mountains. From this he was led to propose a theory of the origin of mountain belts which, though subsequently elaborated and extended, has not since been superceded.

The history of the Appalachians to which Hall addressed himself, and that of the Rocky Mountains as well, begins with the start of the Paleozoic era, half a billion years ago, and with whatever events it was that caused the seas to encroach on the continental platform. The invasion was far-reaching. By the end of the first period of the Paleozoic—the Cambrian—the eastern half of the country, up to about the Canadian border, and large parts of the Southwest had been covered and sediments deposited on the basement rocks. In northern Arizona these deposits were at least twelve hundred feet thick, first of mud and sand, then, as the sea spread farther and the water deepened, of calcareous shells, as we know because these materials formed the rocks of the Tonto Platform of the Grand Canyon.

In the next period of the Paleozoic—the Ordovician, between 425 and 500 million years

ago—the seas advanced even farther, over most of New York and into southern Ontario as well as from the Hudson Bay area almost down to Lake Superior. For about fifty million years, possibly even longer, fully half the entire continent was inundated. Where the Appalachians stand today there was only a shallow trough, and this was perhaps true of much of the site of the Rocky Mountains as well. The seas achieved their maximum conquest during Ordovician times, but for the remainder of the Paleozoic period they alternately moved in over the continental platform and over much of their earlier deposits and retreated again. Mud laid down in the area through which the Niagara River now flows was converted into shale and then overlaid with dolomite-limestone after a later incursion, so that today the water of Niagara Falls, continually excavating the weakly bedded shale from under the lip of the hard capping rock, undermines the latter and causes it to break off; thus we have the rare phenomenon of a falls migrating upstream. In the shallow seas of the mid-Paleozoic periods reefs like turrets or big, thick walls were built up by lime-secreting organisms, chiefly coral and algae, in the region of the northeastern states and Alberta, as in later Paleozoic times such reefs took form in central Texas and, greatest of all, in western Texas. (They are of more than academic interest since petroleum is often found trapped in reservoirs in their vicinity.) During what is known as the Mississippian period (between 310 and 345 million years ago), another time of far-reaching encroachment by the sea, limestone over two thousand

feet thick, destined to play an important part in the later topography of the country, was laid down over a vast area between Alaska and Arizona and between the sites of the Rockies and of the Appalachians.

It may be that in any descent from the Appalachians across the plateau to the interior lowlands you have occasion to feel the reality of those Paleozoic seas. You certainly have in traversing Tennessee on Interstate 40. About a hundred miles on the other side of Knoxville the highway begins to dip into sandstone strata—beaches of seas that withdrew from shores along here over 200 million years ago. A few miles farther on, in deeply hewn terrain, it drops about five hundred feet through successive vertical cuts in level strata of sandstone and dark shale, stacked thirty feet deep, some of the shale almost purple. And from here on to the Tennessee River at the edge of the coastal plain, seventy-five miles beyond Nashville, the highway continues periodically to descend as down a long series of steps, each time through deep cuts. (The easy gradients of the Interstate system are prodigal of the taxpayer's money and usually of land as well, but the cuts do yield instructive and exciting geological exhibits—which would be much more profitable if motorists were provided interpretations.)

One, where the highway drops to the Caney Fork River, stands over a hundred feet high, a sheer wall of course upon course of strata from an inch to several feet in thickness. For 160 miles, through the choppy topography of the plateau, through woods and farmland, you pass periodically between these walls, the rock becoming prevailingly of pale blue-grey or nearly white limestone, the strata tilting down to the west. Where a river like the Caney Fork has cut a deep course through the hills, the overgrown walls are like fortifications in a jungle that has been forgotten by time. Like all ruins, they haunt you.

Above everything, they bring back the seas of which they formed the bottom—the wash of the waves on the beach, the tide running out past mud flats. You can almost see the salt grasses rippling and hear the cries of the gulls, and you have to remind yourself that there was nothing resembling grasses or birds when this was sea. The sediments of which the rocks on the approaches to Nashville were formed were deposited by seas in which the first vertebrates—primitive, armored fishes—were just beginning to appear. These are Ordovician strata and older than any exposed around them; here the continental basement has been domed upward, raising the surface rocks, from which the topmost, young layers have been planed off by erosion. Similar upwarps have resulted in the exposure of these 400-million-year-old strata also in the Frankfort-Cincinnati dome to the north and across the Mississippi in the Ozark highlands. Trilobites, to which the nearest living relative today is the horseshoe crab, dominated the Ordovician seas, which they shared with the protozoans, sponges, corals, brachiopods (somewhat like mussels), squids, nautiluses, sea urchins, and crinoids (which resemble attenuated starfish on plant-like stems). The land upon which the waves broke was one of utter desolation. Algae

did not venture forth upon the shore to produce the first land-plants—abject, protoferns resembling liverworts—until the next period, the Silurian.

For 300 million years, seascapes rather than landscapes were characteristic of the eastern part of our country and probably of most of the western portion of the whole continent as well—that is, for a stretch of time half again as long as that which has followed it. And it was to be far longer than 300 million years before substantially all the country as we know it today was to stand above the sea. During those millions of centuries sediments were washing into the trough from which the Appalachians were to arise. Ultimately the accumulations were miles thick, up to twelve or fifteen times as thick as those laid down inland of the trough. As James Hall observed, it was impossible that the sea had been miles deep (or anything like it) where the accumulations took place. The only logical inference was that the bottom sagged beneath the deposits as they were built up—probably in water never deeper than that covering the continental shelf today.

As for the origin of the sediments, that is a nice question, and one with fascinating ramifications. The deposits on the inner, or western, side of the trough, of which the sedimentary-rock Appalachians were to be formed, consisted initially of sand and silt which could have been carried in from a considerable distance. These were followed by the calcareous deposits of marine organisms up to nine thousand feet thick. So far, so good. But later deposits were of sand, silt, and gravel clearly washed in from

land on the *eastern* side. The direction from which the deposits came is established by the principle that water carries fine particles farther than heavy ones from the place of origin. The material deposited on the outer, or eastern, side of the trough included vast amounts of lava mostly erupted underwater. But most of it, like that on the other side of the trough, was of the products of the disintegration of rocks which could have been carried in only by streams issuing from the east. Indeed, the Appalachians are largely composed of the deltas of rivers flowing in from the direction of what is now the coastal plain and the Atlantic Ocean. Included in them were coarse materials and poorly sorted sediments which could have been laid down only by streams tumbling steeply down from the highlands. Yet nothing is known of any nearby lands on the east that could have supplied the sediments that went into the Appalachians.

Until the past few years the existence of a now-vanished land named Appalachia was hypothesized to account for those sediments, but in the area which we are constrained to believe it would have had to occupy there is only suboceanic crust and nothing resembling the foundations of a sunken portion of the continent. One later hypothesis is that volcanic island arcs, like those in the Pacific today, and ridges from earlier sedimented troughs were raised up and rapidly worn down. More daringly, and perhaps more satisfyingly, it has been suggested that the source of the sediments bulked vastly larger than that—that it was nothing less than Western Europe.

THE APPALACHIANS: II

The theory that the continents were once joined was advanced by Alfred Wegener, a German, in 1912 and at about the same time by an American, Frank Bursley Taylor. The theory holds that the Appalachians are composed in large part of material carried down from the mountains we know once existed in Europe.

Of mountain ranges on either side of the Atlantic that look as if they might once have been continuations of each other, the Appalachians and those of northwestern Europe are not the only examples. The Cape Ranges of South Africa and the Serra do Mar of Brazil would seem to match up, as would the Atlas Mountains of North Africa and the ranges of Guiana and Venezuela.

But there is much to support the theory of continental dispersion in addition to this apparent continuity of mountain belts. The parallelism of the Atlantic's opposite shores (by which actually is meant the edges of the continental shelves) and the submerged Mid-Atlantic Ridge would seem too close for coincidence. Given a natural order strongly disposed to symmetry, the irregular, broken outlines of the landmasses suggest fragments of a larger body in a state of flux. In South America and Africa the oldest fossil-bearing rocks are of about the same age (mid-Paleozoic); the fossils they contain resemble each other while differing from those elsewhere. Dinosaur tracks of Mesozoic river bottoms in England match those of Mesozoic muds of the Connecticut River valley. Of the three surviving genera of lungfish— "living fossils"—one each is found in South

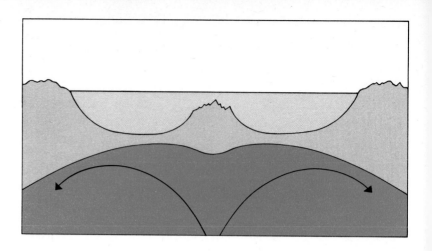

America, Africa, and Australia. Shallow-water organisms, land-plants, and animals on one side of the ocean resemble those on the other. Most of the world's major orders of living things are widely distributed among the continents, and it would seem strange if the land-bridges, floating logs, and sinking continents could have accomplished their spread while having failed to transport any of the higher mammals to Australia (which has only the early evolved marsupials) or New Zealand (which has no indigenous mammals). If the dispersionists are right, these landmasses must have been among the first to be isolated from the proto-continent.

Three other pieces of evidence would seem almost to clinch the case for dispersion. One relates to an epochal event in the Southern Hemisphere of late Paleozoic times, which we shall come to later. Another has to do with the polarity of molecules in rocks. These, when the rock is still molten, tend to act as compass needles and point to the poles. But in bedrock in various parts of the world the molecules have been found pointing in other directions. Unless we take it that the poles have shifted position since the rocks hardened—and impossible wanderings on their part would be required to account for the variances—we must believe that the rock-bearing lands have done so. The third witness to the migration of the continents is the pattern of magnetism of the ocean's floor. This has been found to be made up on either side of virtually all the mid-oceanic ridges of parallel, symmetrically arranged stripes, implying that the crust has been moving away from the central part of the ridges in both directions.

Heretofore, the great objection to the theory of continental dispersion has been the apparent lack of any operating force equal to moving such enormous bodies. But if a theory that geologists have recently evolved proves sound, that objection will have been removed. As it is, most geologists would probably agree with Peter Furneaux Friend of Cambridge University, who, on the subject of continental movement, recently contended that the "evidence has accumulated to establish beyond a reasonable doubt that this drift has indeed occurred" and that attention "should now be turned from the question of *whether* drift has occurred to the manner in which it *has* occurred."

Whatever the source of the Appalachians' ingredients, these accumulated in the sagging trough to thicknesses of up to five miles in the outer, eastern part. James Hall, describing the phenomenon, reasoned that as the strata of solidified sediments sagged, compression folded them and magma at great depths invaded them, setting the stage for the next phase—the elevation of the folded rocks and the plutonic bodies within them into mountains. In broad outlines his theory remains unchallenged as describing the origin of all folded-mountain belts, which includes the Rockies, Alps, Andes, and Himalayas as well as the Appalachians.

The man who took issue with Hall was James Dwight Dana, a professor at Yale, who was one of the great figures of American geology. It was said in tribute to Dana that with him geology became much more than "a chronicle of interesting events . . . it became a philosophical history, a life history, a history of the evolution of the earth." Dana subscribed to the doctrine, long to reign thereafter, that the earth was gradually cooling and hence shrinking. To this process, comparable to the drying out and wrinkling of an apple, he ascribed the elevation of the continents and mountains.

The theory of a shrinking earth has been pretty generally discarded, but the fundamental issue on which Hall and Dana divided is still not fully resolved. Does the crust subside because of the weight of sediments piling up on it, or do sediments accumulate where they do because a trough is formed by forces acting from within the earth? Then there is the related question of what raises the mountains. Are the mechanics those of a log that is dropped into the water and rebounds, albeit in infinitely slow motion? Or is it a matter of the buoyant mountain-forming mass being released from beneath by a relaxation of the internal drag on the sea's bottom, which produced the trough? Geologists seem to be coming to the view that folded-mountain belts owe their existence to the same force that appears to be moving the continents—that is, to the convection currents in the plastic materials of the earth's mantle.

The process, if it is actually at work, is a simple one. The material of the lower part of the mantle heats up, probably because of the heat generated by small amounts of radioactive elements, and this causes it to expand and become lighter than that near the surface. As gravity pulls the latter down, the heated material mushrooms up. The upwellings are like the blisters on the surface of a thick liquid being brought to a boil in a saucepan. As in the saucepan, any scum on the liquid will be pushed away from the blister and collect in the areas between blisters, which are likely to be wrinkled and located where the down-drag is.

In the case of the earth—if the mantle is, in fact, in process of overturn—the blisters are thousands of miles in extent and the movement of rock at their surface is imperceptibly slow —something like half an inch a year. If convection currents perform the role it is now generally believed they do, the mid-oceanic ridges mark the median lines of upwellings, so that the down-drags occur along the continental margins; it is by such means, as by a conveyor belt, that sediments and lavas on the ocean floors may eventually be "welded" onto the continents. The mid-oceanic ridges are places of volcanic activity. Iceland is an outstanding product of such activity along the Mid-Atlantic Ridge, which recently has sprouted two little volcanoes off Iceland's southwest coast.

If convection currents are responsible for forming mountains it is because, first, the down-drag creates the trough in which the sediments collect and pulls them under to depths at which they are metamorphosed, and, secondly, the deceleration of the current stops the drag and allows the transformed sedimentary rock to rise or "float" back up, forming a mountain belt.

Be these things as they may—and they are on the fascinating frontier of geology today— the layered, sedimentary rocks of which the

Appalachians were to be created sank to unknown depths and, before they emerged as mountains, were buckled, folded, and forced over one another. There is no doubt about that, but there is doubt as to how it came about. The conventional explanation asks us to visualize a carpet being compressed laterally and, in consequence, rising in folds. But rock strata are not woven textiles. What lateral compression would have done to them would presumably have been to pulverize their sides or mash them, depending on whether they behaved as a solid or plastically. It seems fair to say that nothing could have folded the strata but a force operating along their whole extent. And the only such force identifiable is gravity.

Compression and folding could have taken place as the trough deepened and its sides became steeper; the strata along the slope would have tended to slip down it and then to have buckled into folds—while above, the strata would have been stretched out. Compression and folding could also have taken place as the floor of the trough was rising, which would have narrowed the space they occupied.

In any case, the conditions in the regions in which these events proceeded (and proceeded with a deliberateness unreckoning of thousands of millennia) are appalling to think upon. There were the inconceivable pressures on the rock in the earth's relentless and tightening embrace. There were the convulsive jerks as groaning strata yielded to mounting strains and snapped, jarring the surrounding regions and sending hundred-foot waves racing through the sea at five miles a minute to break with shattering violence on shores perhaps on the other side of the planet. There were dislocations deep in the mantle from which magma was released: sometimes to well up through cracks in the rock above or to spread between the strata, perhaps forcing them asunder in mountain-sized blisters; sometimes pouring through rents to flood the floor of the sea; sometimes to be coughed up through the maws of volcanoes above it.

On the eastern side of the trough the strata were thickest and the depression greatest. Here the rocks were also subjected to extremely high temperatures, occasioned in part by the temperature of the depths to which they were drawn down, and in part by friction as the tortured strata, like gritted teeth in a bite of demonic force, were dragged past one another. At the same time, many strata were permeated by superheated fluids of diverse ingredients from adjacent regions. The result was that their component minerals were recrystallized or were decompounded and their constituent chemicals recombined or combined with added chemicals to form new minerals.

By these processes of transformation, known collectively as metamorphism, rocks of one kind become rocks of another, and sometimes of so different a kind that the nature of the original can only be guessed at. Quartz sandstone becomes the very hard, sugary-textured rock of interlocking crystals called quartzite. Shale becomes slate. Through further degrees of metamorphism, shale, slate, and graywacke (a sedimentary rock of mixed sand and mud and sometimes gravel) are transformed into

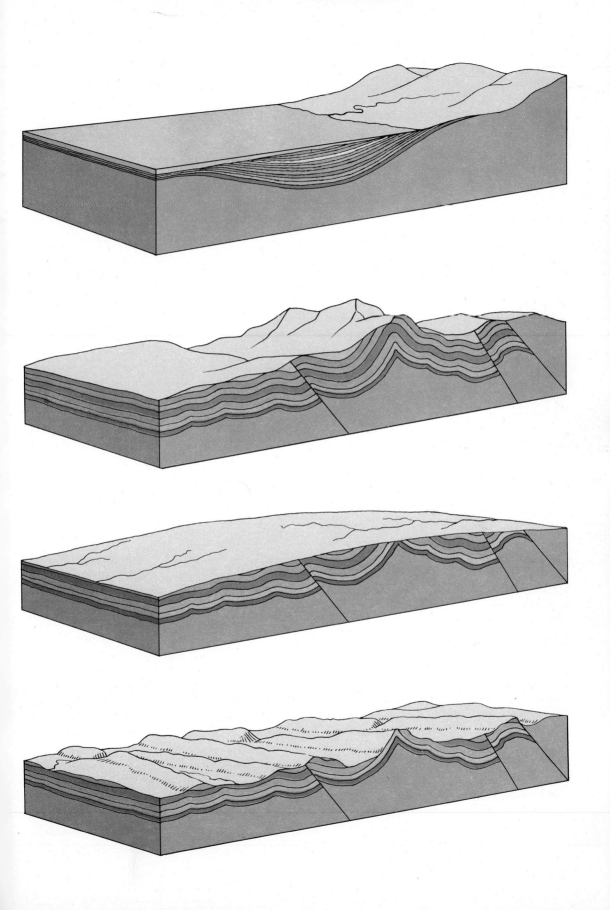

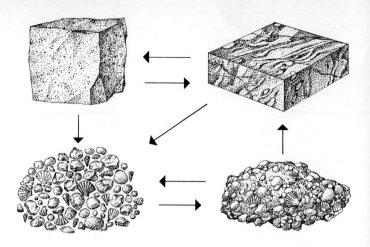

one of the varieties of schist. So may lava be.

Gneiss (pronounced "nice") is the highly metamorphosed rock derived from shales, schists, or even from granite and its allies. What chiefly differentiates it is that the minerals of which it is formed come in relatively large crystals (and in this, as in its ingredients, gneiss resembles granite) and tend to be segregated by type in bands that are noticeably different in color but not sharply defined.

From the loosest sediment through the most granite-like gneiss, a complete gradation exists. The origin of metamorphic rocks that make up a large part of mountain belts is well established, but what about the huge granite bodies ensconced in them? It was once assumed that these were formed of granitic magma that had come up from the depths and had replaced the sedimentary rock that it invaded. What the assumption leaves unexplained, however, is where all that magma could come from, and what happens to the rock it displaces. These difficulties do not seem trivial when we think in terms of the Sierra Nevada, a granite batholith nearly four hundred miles long, seventy-five miles wide, and God knows how deep.

Could the displaced sedimentary rock itself be the origin of the granite? That granite is not necessarily igneous but may be produced by metamorphism is demonstrated by the way in which known metamorphic rocks grade piecemeal into granitic. Undoubtedly much granite is created from rock of lower grade down where high temperatures and pressures rule. There is, it would seem, warrant for believing that rock goes through a regular cycle by which the products of granite's decomposition, reformed as sedimentary rock, pass through progressive metamorphism, eventually to be recreated as granite in batholiths or smaller bodies, and ultimately to reappear once more in lofty summits. There is also reason to believe that this process accounts in a major way for the constitution of the great mountain belts. Combined with the regularity with which sediments carried out to sea are restored to the continents, the transformation would testify most persuasively to an unfailing economy and self-renewing orderliness in nature.

The Appalachians did not, when their time came, break forth dripping from the sea. Their rise can only have been imperceptible, with erosion taking its toll as their uplift proceeded. It may have begun with ranges extending from the Texas Panhandle eastward through southern Oklahoma and on into central Arkansas, where today their remnants—the Arbuckle, Wichita, and Ouachita ranges—are considered an extension of the Appalachians.

By the end of the Mississippian period, about 310 million years ago, the forged-rock Appalachians (those, that is, with igneous and metamorphic rocks as prime constituents) had as a whole been elevated well above sea level. ("Mississippian" is a term that exemplifies the uninspired practice, adopted by geologists long ago, of naming periods of time after geographical areas with which they had no more connection than with others.) On the interior side, between the growing mountain barrier on the east and the gently rising ground on the north and west, a basin was formed from which the sedimentary-rock Appalachians and the Appalachian Plateaus were later to rise. Scanning the interior lowlands beyond the basin, one would have seen others like it, long and broad, set apart from one another by uplifted portions of the continental surface, into which streams also flowed. These basins became for long eras the site of vast freshwater swamps. A year-round, subtropical climate prevailed over all North America and Europe; even Greenland was verdant—and this is perhaps additional evidence that the position of the continents was different in the past from what it is today. Favored by setting and climate, the vegetation of the swamps may have been as luxuriant as any the world has seen.

There had dawned the 25-million-year period called the Pennsylvanian (another unfortunate designation), in which the world's major coal fields were to come into being.

The prostrate little proto-ferns of the mid-Paleozoic had in the course of 100 million years evolved into trees as much as a hundred feet tall and four feet or more through the butt. There were seed-bearing tree ferns and—pointing the way to the forests of the future—primitive conifers with long, strap-like leaves. In forests astir with millepedes, spiders, scorpions, cockroaches up to four inches long, and dragonflies of thirty-inch wing spread, and among which a variety of amphibians shuffled, the trees and the understory of ferns grew and died and their remains piled up—trunks, leaves, spores, and seeds.

The end of it might have been nothing more than exceptionally deep muck had the accumulating beds of decaying vegetable matter not been periodically covered by marine sediments as the seas reinvaded or by freshwater silts as rivers from the rising highlands spread their deltas over them. The effect was to compact the beds of plant tissue and inhibit their decay in such a way as to preserve in an elemental state much of the carbon they contained. Thus was coal produced, with varying proportions of carbon, in accordance with which we grade it today. Where coal occurs, it forms layers interbedded with strata of shale, sandstone, or limestone, the total accumulation sometimes many thousands of feet thick.

Coal fields originating in the Pennsylvanian period underlie a wide area of Illinois, Indiana, western Kentucky, and another area extending from Iowa to central Texas. But the major accumulations are those on the inland side of the Appalachians from Pennsylvania southward. These once spread much farther east, but the coal beds in the subsequently folded strata, converted by heat and pressure from bituminous to high-carbon anthracite, were eroded away following the uplift of the strata, except for the valuable veins in eastern Pennsylvania.

If the folding of the strata that went into the forged-rock Appalachians took place in the abyss of the trough, the folding of those on the west that created the sedimentary-rock Appalachians must have taken place as the former ranges arose and, like a fist pushing up from under the side of a stack of pancakes, gave them a tilt to the west, causing them to slide in that direction and buckle. This is indicated by the fact that the displacement of the strata was

toward the west and that the folds lean in that direction, in some cases having flopped entirely over to the west to lie on their sides. In Pennsylvania the strata were accordioned by as much as 25 or 30 per cent, and to the south the foreshortening was even greater. From Virginia into Tennessee, folds could not take up the compression; the strata ruptured and the part on the east of the break overrode that on the west by miles. Some of these thrust faults are hundreds of miles long. One can imagine the earthquake when a layer of hard rock hundreds of feet thick snapped along such a zone.

The mountain-rearing movement, progressing from the right-hand side of the trough to the left, seems to have consumed tens of millions of years between the first uplift and the raising of the sedimentary-rock Appalachians and the plateaus. By that time the long Paleozoic era was ending, bringing in the first of the dinosaurs, which were about eight feet long and bipedal, to behold the Appalachians in their pristine majesty.

What can hardly be doubted is that they were a mighty mountain belt indeed, of jagged peaks perpetually snowcapped, comparable in elevation to the Alps today. They extended no one knows exactly how far south and seem to have had spurs running not only through Arkansas and Oklahoma but as far west as the Southern Rockies of Colorado (in which apparently Appalachian rocks have been re-uplifted) and through southwestern Texas, where an outcrop of the sedimentary-rock Appalachians may be recognized between the Pecos and Rio Grande. From Newfoundland, if the support-

ing evidence is to be trusted, they ran in one direction up what is now the east coast of Greenland and through Scotland to the North Cape of Norway and in another through southern England and northern France across Germany. If western Texas and Saxony were by no means as far apart then as now, it still took no inconsiderable range to connect them.

The Appalachians as we know them are the creation of two million centuries of weathering. During such an eternity erosion should have sufficed to wear them down to the gentle relief of the Piedmont six or eight times over. One is forced to the conclusion that the Appalachians have risen enormously since the prolonged period of their original elevation.

During the Mesozoic, the "middle-life" period that succeeded the Paleozoic, sediments in volumes past all conception were carried down from the Appalachian heights to spread out over the interior lowlands and to form a coastal plain to the east and south. Some filled troughs in the ranges themselves. The most distinctive of these formed long beds of the well-known "Triassic red sandstone," of which innumerable buildings have been constructed. To give an idea of the scale of this peripheral feature of the great erosional process, it might be mentioned that the Triassic beds in central Connecticut are almost three miles thick. (Deposition of the sandstone, incidentally, was interrupted three times by floods of lava. Such floods occurred also during the deposition of the great red sandstone belt that crosses north-central New Jersey and the southeastern corner of Pennsylvania. One of them created a

huge sill, like a tabletop a thousand feet thick, of which the cut-away eastern edge is the Palisades, the famous cliff along the western shore of the Hudson River.)

What happened when rock layers up to two or three miles in thickness were stripped off the Appalachians was what happens to an iceberg as it melts down from the top. The remains of the range rose by an amount proportionate to the weight of which they had been relieved. (The principle is the one that geologists term isostasy—"equal station." It holds that as weight is added to or removed from a section of the earth's crust, that section will gradually sink or rise proportionately, so that all parts of the planet's surface will be maintained in a rough equilibrium.) A view commonly met with is that before the rise occurred the range had been worn down to a peneplain (an almost-plain) traversed by sluggish, meandering rivers with mountains of resistant rock standing some hundreds of feet above it. According to this view the re-elevation of the terrain set the rivers and the streams that fed them to coursing once more down steep declivities and to carving out a new topography, sculpturing mountains of hard rock and excavating valleys where the rock was weaker—thus the Appalachians that have come down to us today.

But is this necessarily the way it was? There are those who do not find the explanation convincing, who feel that the uplift of the range would more nearly have kept pace with its reduction and the Appalachians never have lost their mountainous contours. There is no argument, however, about some of the reasons for the present character of the range. Why the Appalachian Plateaus should have a configuration so maddening to anyone who sets out to overcome them is fairly evident. Uplifted more or less *en masse* with little distortion of their strata, they were carved up haphazardly by water ferreting out paths of least resistance to the lowlands. In the case of both the plateaus and the sedimentary-rock Appalachians, the presence of thick, underlying layers of limestone had a good deal to do with the outcome. Streams traversing the plateaus slowly dissolved the limestone. Many vanished underground, flowing for long distances before gushing out as springs on lower hillsides. In the Cumberland Plateau, as in the limestone regions of Indiana and Michigan, the surface was undermined in places and collapsed in sinks.

In the sedimentary Appalachians, where the strata were turned up in windrows, the limestone was leached away, leaving the upper layers of the less soluble shale and sandstone as the crests of ridges. Where the turning up was by folding, the limestone was exposed by the decapitation of the folds by gradual erosion. Where there was thrust-faulting in place of folding, we can visualize what happened by imagining the sides of a boardwalk squeezed together in such a way as to cause each plank to override its neighbor on the west and turn up, bringing the edge of its lower part into view. In both cases, the reduction of the limestone by weathering and solution and the persistence of the shale and sandstone left an alternation of long, narrow, even ridges and corresponding flat valleys.

On the eastern side of the ridge-and-valley province, as it is called, the crustal rocks were raised higher by the upthrust of the forged-rock Appalachians, and a wide platform of limestone was uncovered—wide and deep, for the strata here were much compressed laterally. The outcome of eons of leaching in this zone was the Great Valley of the Appalachians, and, as underground rivulets seeped through fissures in the remaining limestone foundations, the gradual dissolving out of great caverns.

To produce caverns that are galleries of sculptured forms, such as attract throngs of visitors today, the strata from which they were hollowed out had subsequently to be lifted above the water table, so-called, or the table depressed below them, so that erosion would be supplemented by its opposite: deposition. The awe and wonder these lofty, echoing grottoes and labyrinthine passageways excite in us are intensified by the knowledge that the icicles of stone pendant from the cavern's roof, often intricately formed, and the inverse icicles that rise from the floor to meet them, are the creations of water droplets that, one by one, while beading the tips of these concretions or, falling, gave up their ghosts on those below, left behind a microscopic film of calcium carbonate picked up in the limestone above.

Another curiosity of the central sector of the Appalachians, and one that has long excited speculation, is the contrary way in which the rivers that drain it have taken courses athwart the grain of the land. The tributaries behave as one would expect, flowing parallel with one another, often meandering, down the long valleys, but the main stems cut directly across the ridges on their way to the southeast. In the case of the Delaware, Susquehanna, and Potomac there are spectacular water gaps where they break through to the Piedmont.

The chief appeal of the view that the Appalachians were once worn down to a peneplain is that it seems to explain the mountain-breaching rivers. These, it is said, follow roughly the same courses today that they once followed across the plain. Simply, as the uplift took place, they cut their way across the emerging ridges at the same rate at which their tributaries dug valleys out of the limestone strata between the ridges.

Actually, we do not require the peneplain to get the rivers through the ridges. The rivers need not have worn a passage from west to east. They could have done the job in reverse, from east to west. A stream descending from highlands invariably cuts its way back into them. As it inches up toward the ultimate source of its flow, at the top of its watershed, the crumbling of the sides of the cleft it is carving will eventually begin to pluck soil and rocks from the ridge crest—that is, the divide—just behind it. Ultimately the ridge will be breached and the breach enlarged and the stream begin to collect the flow from what has been the watershed on the other side of the divide, "capturing," as the geologists say, the streams that had formerly carried the runoff of the watershed in another direction. So it may be that the rivers of the central Atlantic states wore their channels from the slopes above the Piedmont back into the mountains. And hav-

ing captured the streams that once drained the valleys to some other outlet, they may now be moving against one another. The tributaries of the Potomac, digging their way southward up the higher ground at the head of the Shenandoah Valley, are believed destined to carve their way through and capture the headwaters of the James River.

We shall never, alas, know how the Appalachians looked at the height of their glory. Some of the subsidiary ranges of today, like the Great Smokies, may have been comprised in a single great ridge rising to a height three times that of its tallest existing member. The Appalachian belt may have extended eastward to the outer edge of today's Piedmont, occupying the whole inner half of the present southeastern states—and more. All we can be sure of is that sedimentary strata amounting in thickness to many times the height of the tallest man-made structures have been stripped from the forged-rock Appalachians.

They had to be, for metamorphic rock and granite are never formed except under such a cover, and it is rocks of these kinds that now stand exposed in the highlands of New England and of Canada's Maritime Provinces, in the Blue Ridge, and in the Piedmont. Even the casual motorist crossing the Green Mountains between Burlington and Montpelier on Interstate 89 can hardly overlook the special character of the rocks revealed in the new, deep cuts. There are grey gneisses marbled by veins of white quartz, as beef is marbled by veins of fat, and slaty schists that divide into plates resembling silvered pewter. (Schists generally do not

seem very strong, but schist—and schist from older mountains than the Appalachians—supports the heaviest mass of buildings in the world, in Manhattan Island.) At Montpelier you are offered a tour of the world's largest granite quarry, and granite is what the White Mountains are primarily made of.

These are also the principal rocks you see in the eastern Appalachians of the South along the Skyline Drive and Blue Ridge Parkway—except that for long stretches in Virginia the embankments are of a dull, neutral green rock, heavy and fine-grained, that fractures in knife-sharp edges. This is greenstone, a metamorphosed basalt that takes us back before the time when the Appalachian range was a slowly filling trench. Unfortunately greenstone and the lively grey schists and gneisses weather to drab browns. The rock in the older cuts along the parkway might be coffee-stained; you would hardly glance at it a second time. The highest rocks in the eastern United States are weathered garnet schist and quartz-feldspar gneiss, side by side, at the topmost foot or two of Mount Mitchell.

The huge granite outcrops along the eastern Appalachians and Piedmont have been found to run in age from 185 million years in New England to 400 million years in the South. As long ago as that the range we still have very much with us today was already in gestation in the crucible of the depths. These are indeed old mountains. They look their age, too, and perhaps most of all, surely most movingly, in spring. Then the grey, worn rocks commanding their treeless summits or obtruding through the forest floor of their slopes, are host to wafers of lichen, curls of rock tripe, and polypodium fern nestled in their crevices, or stand guardian to pink and white trillium, lavender-pink beds of wild geranium, clumps of lavender-blue field violets, flame azalea, mountain laurel, or the flowering rhododendrons that stand forty feet high in hollows they render impenetrable or crouch in wind-sheered mats on the ridges as far north as the Catskills.

Writing in 1818 of the mountains on the Virginia-Tennessee border, the author of a paper in the first volume of the *American Journal of Science* observed that they seem to have lain for ages in undisturbed repose, exhibiting "none of the remarkable appearances which indicate the changes and convulsions which have been wrought by time, the great enemy of nature." Almost, it is true, one has the impression that the Appalachians have come through the province of time altogether. The streams, to be sure, continue to abrade their beds, if slowly, and if the vegetation that cloaks them tends to build them higher by continuing deposits of humus, the slippage of soil and rock detritus on the steeper slopes, called "sag," tends to reduce them. But if the principle of isostasy is reliable, mountains, as long as they *are* mountains, must be rising from below as they are being lowered from above. And if their bases extend thirty or forty miles down to begin with, they have it in them to do a prodigious lot of rising. The Appalachians, which surely must still have large reserves to draw upon, will be here for a long time to come—and in human terms, forever.

THE ROAD WEST

Commenting on the difficulties the pioneer geologists had encountered in the East, where a vastly eroded topography masked by vegetation had to be deciphered without the microscope, analytical chemistry, or innumerable other later scientific aids, a biographer of James Dwight Dana was led to "wonder what would have been the history of American geology if the earlier workers in it could have started their labors in our West." What the West meant to him was: "magnificent exposures; structural geology cleanly displayed on a large and evident scale; stratigraphic series laid open to observation; every stage from intrusive to extrusive effects of volcanic energy bared by dissection. . . ."

All the same, one cannot quit the East and turn to the West without regretting the essential simplicity of what one is leaving behind. The Appalachian Range is a model of a folded-mountain belt. Everything is there; nothing has been added to confuse the issue. The West intimidates by the complexity of its geology just as it lures by the grandeur of its forms.

Crossing the continent from the older part of the country, you find that the West comes by stages. Perhaps its first onset is most abrupt if your route lies through the Ouachita Mountains, south of the Arkansas River beyond Little Rock. In this way you hold on to the end to the bright green, richly varied deciduous forest of the East. Not only in natural cover, but in form as well, the Ouachitas recall the parallel ridges of the sedimentary-rock Appalachians, of which they are probably an extension.

Descending from the hills to cross into

In 1804 under Government auspices Captain Meriwether Lewis (right) and Lieutenant William Clark (left) began their exploratory trip from the mouth of the Missouri northwestward to the Pacific, 4,134 miles away. Their trip, of which President Jefferson wrote, "Never did a similar event excite more joy thro' the United States," also established the role of the Government in promoting and funding scientific research.

Oklahoma at Fort Smith, you find within half an hour you have left the South and entered a different world. Except for the Ouachitas petering out in the distance on the left, the land is flat and open. As you cross Oklahoma it begins to take on the aspect of an ocean, its undulations like a calm sea's majestic swells. There is wheat on the uplands and cottonwoods nestled in clumps in the troughs.

The main north-south Oklahoma-Texas border is the 100th meridian. It is a crucial dividing line because it marks the beginning, roughly, of the short-grass plains and of a different climate. In the West, precipitation in the high mountains would by eastern standards be called light to moderate. From northern California northward it is heavy on the Coast Ranges and drenching along the extreme littoral and in the Olympics. But elsewhere, from the leading edge of the Great Plains westward, drought is an omnipresent fact of life.

Another change takes place here too. Since leaving the Mississippi alluvial plain in central Arkansas, you have been traveling over deposits of later Paleozoic times, 220 to 250 million years ago. Now suddenly you are on deposits no more than twelve million years old—the outwash of the young western mountains. Though you cannot discern it, the land is gaining constantly in elevation, about ten or twelve feet in every mile. With Texas its sweep is greater and the color prevailingly dun. There is a bleakness about it, as of land back from the seashore dunes, and it is a realm over which sun and wind reign as absolute monarchs.

By driving for only an hour into the state, a portentous though initially insignificant phenomenon may be observed. Steep-sided ditches snaking through the reddish, gravelly soil are the beginnings of what, five hundred miles farther on, will be dizzy chasms. And you do not have to wait long for the cuts to expand. Twenty miles short of New Mexico on the road from Amarillo you spot the first of those abrupt escarpments characteristic of the West, in which a tableland formed of the products of erosion has been cut down by further erosion to a lower level in a cliff fifty or a thousand feet high with a profile like a plowshare's. (Two such escarpments face to face give you a canyon. Back to back and at a considerable distance apart they form a *mesa*, the Spanish word for table. When closer together they form a *butte*, a French word originally connoting a goal or boundary, an endpiece. Mesas tend to be reduced to buttes and buttes to chimneys or pinnacles.) This severe cutting away of the land comes about where the rainfall is sufficient when concentrated in thunderstorms to wear away the softer sedimentary rocks but insufficient to provide for protective vegetation.

Dropping down to the flat valley of the Canadian River, you behold the ruined edges of the Great Plains to the south as a series of escarpments like massive headlands standing out to sea. There is a sudden abundance of a shrub with pale green, pinnate leaves like a locust's but finer—mesquite. Where the road skirts the front of a mesa you can see that the top of the formation is armored by a great plate of sandstone; the mesa is cut back as the sandstone is undermined and falls away in chunks. Sand-

stone—great buff-colored blocks of it—also forms the brows of the ridges that, one upon another, lead off to the south like a flotilla of super-dreadnoughts.

In descending to the Canadian River valley you have dropped from late Cenozoic rocks back to those of the early Mesozoic. After crossing the Pecos you go back still further. From the end of the Southern Rockies well into Texas, erosion has exposed rock strata laid down as a sea bottom in late Paleozoic times to a known thickness of over two miles. From here westward the surface rocks are continually changing in age or character or both, for not only has a variety of mountain-rearing processes been at work across the region but unequal erosion has left expanses of new rock in some places and unearthed others tens of millions of years older a mile away.

But if the West's geology is bewildering, you can hardly avoid being transported by the splendor of what is spread before you. The West may take over from the East progressively, but it is likely to reserve the full force of what it has to communicate and then capture the newcomer in one swift coup. This is most apt to happen if, as you approach its redoubts, you quit the main highway for a secondary road that you will have, for spells, to yourself.

There is rolling range to the far distance—let us say that you have turned from the east-west Interstate north toward the Oku Range—"the Turtle," called *Sangre de Cristo* by the Spaniards, who evidently were reminded of blood by the sunset reflected on its snows. It is a silver-tawny grassland on which, dispersed as if by conscious husbandry, are cholla cacti like many-branched staghorns in the velvet and those stocky man-sized trees that defy the drought on the tablelands where no others survive, the fragrant little western junipers. And bounding the plains ahead are long, low, juniper-speckled ridges that have the air of medieval fortresses. You can imagine yourself riding over those plains for hours upon hours, for days. In that immense space made overpowering by its silence, in the solitude of those distances leading to the translucent blue-grey shadow outlining the dark ridges that are the beginning of the West's mighty ramparts, you feel, as if it were the first time in your memory, uncramped.

Thomas Jefferson may be said to have launched the exploration of the West and with it the lasting participation of the United States Government in the furtherance of scientific inquiry. This he did when he sent a party overland to the Pacific in the first transcontinental crossing of the present United States and made sure that one of its primary aims would be the collection of data and specimens covering all the natural sciences.

Like Jefferson, Captain Meriwether Lewis had a mind of a speculative and scientific bent. (Once during an international crisis Jefferson was found spreading a collection of fossils over the White House tables.) "Captain" (actually Lieutenant) William Clark, another Virginian, was a practical-minded frontiersman with an inborn aptitude for natural history and geography. The expedition, which included some forty white men and one Negro slave, set

out from St. Charles, on the Missouri River, north of St. Louis, in May 1804. The party ascended the Missouri to near the present site of Bismarck, North Dakota, where it wintered with the Mandan Indians. In the spring it pressed on up the Missouri to the source of one of its tributaries in southwestern Montana, where it found itself facing the Continental Divide.

The Rocky Mountains had been crossed before, in a nightmare exploit by Alexander Mackenzie in Canada in 1793, but the Rockies were so vastly underestimated in the United States that Lewis and Clark had expected a day's portage to see them through. Instead, the crossing took almost two months, and the explorers nearly left their bones in Idaho's Bitterroot Mountains. Reaching a tributary of the Columbia with the aid of a half-starved tribe of Shoshonis, they descended by canoe to the Pacific, which they reached in November. In September of the following year, 1806, they were back in St. Louis, having been given up for lost by almost everyone but Jefferson. In their trek, totaling 7,690 miles through wholly unknown country, they had endured every kind of danger and hardship and been for two years without supply from the outside. Yet they had lost but two men and had brought back an immense new knowledge of the country, and, especially of its mountain backbone. It was a triumph of farsighted planning and of qualities of character we like to think particularly American—qualities especially on the part of the two leaders, who accomplished the miracle of amicably sharing command as equals. The expedition represented one of the great feats of exploration of all time and undoubtedly the greatest in our own history.

The next comparable Government-sponsored explorations were those led by John Charles Frémont. Born in Savannah in 1813, Frémont had a somewhat Byronic aura about him and united great magnetism with an eager mind, a head for mathematics, and a passion for "travel over a part of the world which remained the new . . . and the study without books—the learning at first hand from nature herself." To these qualities he added technical skills acquired in his twenties in the service of a French scientist-explorer in the upper Mississippi Valley. With an Army commission obtained in the Topographical Engineers, he commanded three expeditions that covered twenty thousand miles in the enormous region between the Mississippi and the Pacific and between the Columbia and the Colorado.

The migration to Oregon and California was well under way in the 1840's, the period of Frémont's surveys, but Frémont did much to abet and facilitate it. Not only did he give the rest of his countrymen a picture of the West unique in its cartographic detail and evocative reporting, but he fired their imaginations as a symbol; his thirty-day crossing of the Sierra Nevada—beset by hardships so severe his Indian guides either deserted or gave themselves up for dead—was superlatively in character. And Frémont was an observer; he could recognize the geological nature of the Great Basin and the agricultural potential of California, as in both cases he was the first to do.

The chief exploratory work conducted by

For the nineteenth-century scientist-explorers who ventured beyond the Mississippi, such awesome spectacles as the Grand Canyon of the Yellowstone (shown below in an 1872 painting by Thomas Moran) provided a view of earth history unlike any they had ever seen. At left is John Charles Frémont, who was among the earliest and most dashing of the expedition leaders to interpret and report on the geologic wonders of the West.

the Government in the next decade was the result of hostilities with the Mexicans that Frémont was instrumental in provoking and which ended with the annexation of California. With the American people firmly established along the West Coast and hundreds more arriving every day, the demand for a transcontinental railroad was insistent. The problem was to find the least difficult route and to reconcile sectional rivalries.

To cope with these rivalries after a number of survey parties had been in the field—the first led by Frémont himself—Congress put the matter in the hands of the Secretary of War, Jefferson Davis. Four parallels were chosen, lying between the 49th and the 32nd, and an expedition with scientists attached sent along each. The odd result was that all four expeditions found feasible routes, which brought the political problem no nearer resolution. A store of new information about the country had been garnered, however, and was published by the Government in a series of quarto volumes. (The question of which route the first railroad would follow was settled by private financiers who in 1860 laid plans to build a line east from Sacramento across the Sierra Nevada, confident that another would come to meet them from the other side of the country. However, in time, railroads were to be put through approximately along each of the four routes explored.)

The surveys for the railroad did not, however, begin to exhaust the Government's avidity for knowledge of the vast country beyond the Mississippi. "A grand national reconnaissance" was "perhaps the chief Western preoccupation of the national government during the era of Manifest Destiny," according to an able historian of the period, William H. Goetzmann. With scientific societies such as the Philadelphia Academy of Natural Sciences and the Smithsonian Institution in Washington supplying trained specialists, "virtually every expedition conducted by the Corps of Topographical Engineers operated under order to make a general examination of plants, animals, Indians, and geological formations of the country traversed."

The Civil War put a crimp in these activities—except in California, where an ambitious state geological survey got under way—but its finish released for field work a body of able young men. These veterans had been spoiled for the routine and confinement of ordinary civilian life and their imaginations required strong fare—large horizons, physical challenge, the variety and uncertainty that add up to adventure, and intellectual objectives to give meaning to hardship and peril. Coincidentally, the realization was growing that geology, even when the motives of geologists were purely scientific, held the key to the efficient exploitation of a country's resources. There had arrived the era of the National Surveys, of which geological discovery was a primary aim.

The longest in the field was the Hayden Survey, launched in 1869, when Congress appropriated funds for Ferdinand V. Hayden to continue and expand the geological exploration he had been conducting for the state of Nebraska. Hayden was a man whose shy, diffident de-

meanor and full beard concealed a remarkable stock of energy, enthusiasm, and perseverance. Born in Massachusetts in 1829, he worked his way through Oberlin College with the intention of becoming a physician. At Albany Medical School, however, he met James Hall, who changed all that. When he graduated in 1853, Hall offered to pay his expenses, and he went on a fossil-collecting trip to the Badlands. The next two years he spent traveling largely on foot in the train of a fur company, his investigations carrying him all the way to the Bighorn River.

This was the country, from the Snake River of Idaho to southern Colorado, that he devoted a quarter of a century to exploring, mapping, and anatomizing, except for the war years, when he served as surgeon of cavalry. As leader of a National Survey for ten years, he sometimes concurrently commanded several parties of as many as thirty members. He and his associates were among the first white men to see the geysers and boiling springs of northwestern Wyoming, and the idea of Yellowstone National Park was born with him. The peoples of the West evidently swore by him—and Federal appropriations for his survey reached the then marvelous sum of $75,000 a year.

But for swaying Congress, nothing could excel the performance of Clarence King, of whom Henry Adams wrote that "no other young American approached him for the combination of chances—physical energy, social standing, mental scope and training, wit, geniality, and science, that seemed superlatively American and irresistibly strong." In 1866, when barely twenty-five, King had presented himself in Washington with a plan for a survey through the widest part of the Cordillera—his term (which geology has adopted) for the whole body of mountains occupying the western third of the country. He argued that not only was a railroad needed to bind California to the nation—it was still only planned—but to enhance its utility the resources of the region should be ascertained and subsequently developed. Within a few months he had won Congressional authorization of the plan and been named geologist-in-charge of the geological exploration of the 40th parallel, under the Secretary of War. The Congressmen had apparently not been put off by his having finessed the late war: Second Bull Run had found him rowing with three friends from Lake Champlain to Quebec; Gettysburg was fought while he was crossing the continent in a wagon train.

The latter expedition led to his crossing the Sierra Nevada on foot and meeting the California Geological Survey. Volunteering with that organization, he spent a year exploring the Sierra, in the course of which he discovered its highest peak—and the highest in the forty-eight states—and named it after the chief of the Survey, W. D. Whitney. His success in Washington came after a tour of duty with an Army expedition in Arizona (in the course of which, in a display of remarkable coolness and ingenuity, he had barely escaped with his life when ambushed and captured by Apaches). The survey of the 40th parallel began in Sacramento in 1868; by the time it had completed its task in the Great Plains in 1872 it had mapped

Western Colorado is shown at left below in one of the highly detailed maps from the Hayden Survey's 1877 Atlas. The "great surveys," as they became known, helped plot the course of the railroads and provided volumes of new information on the geology, geography, and natural history of the West. At right, Hayden (seated at far right) and his party are seen during a momentary pause in their journey through the wilds.

in detail a zone one hundred miles wide and one thousand long. It also produced reports filling seven quarto volumes, of which King wrote a masterly synopsis of eight hundred pages outlining the geological history of the Cordillera, as far as he could divine it.

King, brought up by the widowed young heiress of a merchant family of Newport impoverished by a maritime disaster, had found his lifelong interest at the age of seven in a fossil in the rock of a stone wall. John Wesley Powell, the son of a Methodist preacher, acquired his interest from the master of a tiny school in Ohio, whose specialty was natural history. Born in New York State in 1834, Powell was to bring western exploration to culmination in the same legend of the magnificent hero that Frémont had imparted to it thirty years earlier. His career began in his early twenties with his election to the secretaryship of the Illinois Society of Natural History but was interrupted by the war. An impassioned abolitionist who was later to champion the Red man and the land itself as an early conservationist, Powell volunteered at once and was soon in command of a battery of artillery. Though he lost an arm at Shiloh, he fought through the rest of the war and wound up a major.

The exploit that was to fill in the last significant blank on the map of the United States had its inception when Powell—then a professor of geology and museum director—led a party of students and teachers over the Front Range and up Pikes Peak. A man whose drives of energy, vision, and ambition no classroom or administrator's office could contain, he was in-

stantly responsive when, meeting a fellow veteran of the Union Army, the idea came up of doing what not even the Indians had ever attempted: descending the Colorado River.

On May 24, 1869, the expedition of ten men in four specially constructed boats put off from Green River City in east-central Utah. Three months later, at the entrance to the Black Canyon, southeast of Las Vegas, a family of Mormons who had been asked to keep watch for the wreckage of the boats (that being what was most generally expected to come through) looked up from their fishing to see the boats themselves bearing down on them. The expedition had navigated some nine hundred miles of treacherous waters that flowed, often boiling in ferocious rapids, through gorges with walls up to thousands of feet in height, as high as five thousand in the Grand Canyon. Powell described them as "cliffs and ledges of rock—not such ledges as you may have seen where the quarryman splits his blocks, but ledges from which the gods might quarry mountains . . . and . . . cliffs where the soaring eagle is lost to view ere he reaches the summit." One of the boats had been smashed on a rock early in the trip, but the only lives that had been lost were those of three men who had given up near the end and climbed out of the gorge to return by foot to civilization; they had been waylaid and killed by Indians. In May 1871 Powell set out again with virtually a new party.

That time, taking a cue from King and Hayden, he had a photographer and a painter with him. The leaders in the geological conquest of the West are not, it would seem, to be conceived of as unworldly or as innocent of the value of public relations. However devoted to science, they understood power, were practiced infighters in the jungle of Washington, and were rivals for governmental support.

Another competitor was the Army, which had had the field to itself until the creation of the Hayden Survey in the Department of the Interior. (Powell, nominally under Interior, actually attached himself more to the Smithsonian Institution.) Not to be frozen out, the Army launched the geological surveys west of the 100th meridian under Lieutenant G. M. Wheeler, who endeavored to make up in zeal what he had lost by coming to the scene a generation late. In the space of six months in 1871 his expedition came close to perishing of heat prostration in Death Valley and of exhaustion and hunger while fighting its boats *up*stream in the lower Colorado. However, among the purposes it served in its very wide surveys was one of providing a vehicle for three years for Grove Karl Gilbert, who was perhaps the ablest of all as a geologist. Born in Rochester in 1843, Gilbert had been physically disqualified for war service but was to manage years afield in very trying parts of the country, especially that vast area of the Southwest of "desert valleys between naked ridges," in Powell's words. The "Basin Range system," as Gilbert called it, was his particular province, and he was still refining his analysis of its origins thirty years after his introduction to it. (A droll perspective on himself seems to have been an endearing quality of his. "Among my interesting finds," he wrote then, "are a number of mistakes made

by Gilbert, one of the Wheeler geologists.")

By the late seventies, conflicts among the rival survey groups had reached a pitch that threatened to end Congressional support for any of them. Consolidation was clearly called for. Congress turned for advice to a committee of the National Academy of Sciences. Heavily loaded with friends of King's and Powell's, the committee adopted their proposals. The result was the creation of the United States Geological Survey under the Department of the Interior and also the appointment of King as its first director and of Powell as its second when King resigned a year later. (King was moved by a desire to advance his private fortunes as a mining consultant and it marked the beginning of the deterioration of his career. "He knew more of practical geology," Henry Adams remarked, "than was good for him.") Powell, with Gilbert as his chief geologist, served as director of the Survey, and an energetic and resolute one, until 1894.

As a result of the pioneer surveys, the geology of the West was roughed in, in some cases with remarkable insight. Exploring the ramifications, filling in the details, and working out explanations of what was found has occupied hundreds of geologists ever since—about half of them now employed by the petroleum companies—and is still proceeding; major questions remain unresolved and controversial. However, if the picture at close range seems hopelessly complex and original causes are uncertain, at least it is possible to grasp the kind of events that have created the Cordillera in its manifold forms.

THE ROCKY
MOUNTAINS

It would hardly appear that the Cordillera goes back to anything as straightforward as the origins of the Appalachians. Yet apparently it does. Evidently in the West as in the East there was a trough of continental length flooring a shallow sea in which miles-thick layers of sediments accumulated, starting in early Paleozoic times, and from this trough, as from the other, a great chain of mountains was to arise. The western chain, which was to extend from Alaska southward through Mexico, could be called the Rocky Mountains, with the understanding that most of its remnants today below the northern United States are not called the Rockies and that some mountains that are—the Central and Southern Rockies—do not properly belong to it.

The analogy between the two troughs and their respective histories would seem to be remarkably close. One trough was a mirror image of the other, however. That is, the east side of one corresponded to the west side of the other. With both, it was the inland slope, the side adjacent to the interior lowlands, that was sedimented with silt, sand, and the calcareous shells of marine organisms. With both it was the outer side in which the bulk of the sediments accumulated—sediments that contained coarser materials than those on the inner side as well as great quantities of volcanic rocks derived from upwelling floods of lava and from violent eruptions. And as the great mass of coarse sediments came from the Atlantic side of the Appalachian trough they came from the Pacific side of the Rocky Mountain trough.

As for the source of the sediments in the lat-

Perhaps forty million years ago, long after dinosaurs had disappeared and when mammals were spreading and diversifying, this titanothere (right), a gigantic beast resembling a rhinoceros, roamed a marshy plain that is now the Badlands of South Dakota. Saber-toothed cats, giant pigs, three-toed horses, and tiny camels also roamed the area. Many of them were buried in sediments washing from the still-emerging Rocky Mountains to the west.

ter case, a lost land of "Cascadia" was once conjured up to account for them, analogous to the lost land of "Appalachia." But now both theories appear to have been generally relinquished, giving way to a current view that the sedimentary source was a volcanic island arc arising in a zone of crustal weakness along the outer margin of the trough. Such a ridge would be comparable to the island arcs that stand today along the earthquake-and-volcano belt of the northern and western Pacific—the Aleutian, Kuril, Japanese, Ryukyu and Philippine archipelagoes. It would have had to grow and continue to grow over a very long time. It would have had to be worn down and the spoil of its wearing have been formed into new rocks and these uplifted, in turn, and then decomposed into sediments. But enough time was available—hundreds of millions of years.

The process of deformation, as the geologists call it, that was to create the Rocky Mountains began in mid-Mesozoic times and was similar to that which began in mid-Paleozoic to create the Appalachians. On the outer side of the trough there was the same down-folding of sedimentary strata, the same terrible compression at great depth, the same subjection to high temperatures, the same resultant metamorphism of the rocks, the same creation in the same mysterious fashion of granite batholiths at the core of the fetal range—only here the batholiths were of a magnitude far surpassing anything in the East. The Idaho and Sierra Nevada batholiths are 240 and 300 miles long, respectively, and two in Baja California are also quite long. The Pacific Coast batholith stretches down the entire length of the Alaskan panhandle and Canadian littoral, one monstrous granite body eleven hundred miles in length and with an area of seventy-three thousand square miles. The imagination recoils from the thought of the womb in which these prodigies could have been nursed into being, by whatever process—the same womb in which today, if a million earthquakes a year strong enough to be felt are reliable indicators, other mountain masses are being kneaded and infused with granite to be unveiled half a million or more centuries hence. The granite of the Cordilleran batholiths has been found to be between 80 and 140 million years old.

The location of granitic and metamorphosed rocks indicates that the outer Rocky Mountain trough extended from southern Alaska down the Pacific Coast through Vancouver Island and western Washington into Idaho. There it apparently bent sharply back through Oregon (to raise the Blue Mountains), then to the present coast (where the Klamath Mountains now form a geographical part of the Coast Ranges), whence it ran southeast through western and southern California and western Nevada down Baja California and the west coast of Mexico.

As in the formation of the Appalachians, the mountain-rearing impulse progressed from the outer side of the trough to the inner, in the course of several-score millions of years. Geologists refer to the first phase as the *Nevadan orogeny* (literally, "mountain-making") and to the latter as the *Laramide orogeny*. Again, as the mountains rose on the outer side, erosion

wore off their covering rock and spread the residue over the inner side of the trough and far beyond. Some was carried to the sea that still reached from the Arctic down through Montana and Wyoming, but much greater masses were spread across the land to the south, which had emerged from the sea and was probably desert. These outwashes were later converted to the eolian sandstones (solidified dunes) that are a prominent and often spectacular feature of the Southwest.

It is far from having been one uninterruptedly. During the last period of the Mesozoic, between about 60 and 100 million years ago, it was inundated by a sea that spread from the Gulf of Mexico to the Arctic and from the front of the rising young mountains to the prairie states. This was the period that saw the colossal contents of the Rocky Mountain trough at last altogether emergent. A mighty, mountain-rearing surge held sway from the late Mesozoic on into the Cenozoic, in which we are living today. As in the case of the Appalachians, it was the layers of sedimentary rock on the inland side of the trough that were the last to be affected by the forces of upthrust.

The genesis of a chain of mountains destined to stand among the world's great ranges should, one feels, have been manifested in dramatic and decisive fashion. Evidently it was not. Anyone alive at the time would presumably have been unlikely to notice much change from the time of his earliest memory to that of his death even if his life span had been as long as the entire time in which *Homo sapiens* has been on earth. Fossils indicate that the land to the east of the rising ranges remained a humid one, as it would not have if a barrier had been interposed between it and the sources of rain in the Pacific. The inference is that the ranges were at most only a few thousand feet above the basin and were reduced by erosion about as fast as they were raised. Along their front, which followed a line down through central Utah and central Arizona, the deposits accumulated to depths of nearly three miles; Pikes Peak would have disappeared in them without a trace. It can only be that the crustal rocks sank through their own weight. Conditions must have been much as they were on the corresponding side of the Appalachians during the period of the great coal forests, for today extensive coal fields run through here from central Alberta down into northwestern New Mexico, with smaller coal fields extending up through Alaska.

But the plants of these coal swamps were not those of the coal swamps of the East. The plants of Pennsylvanian times had been displaced primarily by the cycads, which look like palms but are more related to the conifers and ginkgos. Both these latter were also plentiful in the late Mesozoic, including the forerunners of the Sequoias. With the Cenozoic came the first of the modern trees—sycamores, magnolias, sassafras, oaks, and willows, as well as true palms. The transition from one great age to the other, which saw the process that was raising the sedimentary Rocky Mountains—the Laramide orogeny—at its most intense, was a time of revolutionary change.

The Mesozoic, the Age of Reptiles, had

reached its zenith in Cretaceous times: brontosaurs, eighty feet in length and weighing as much as fifty tons, foraged in the swamps; tyrannosaurs, which could have yanked a man from a third-floor window in their jaws and were doubtless the most fearsome engines of destruction the planet has ever seen, would have shaken the earth when they ran; ostrich-like pterosaurs sailed above the sea on wings that spread twenty-seven feet.

To share the seas with Pteranodon there were already early water birds: the toothed Hesperornis, representing a reversion to flightlessness, and several species of Ichthyornis, rather loon-like birds in the guise of terns. Now came the ancestors of ibises, flamingos, and cormorants, soon to be followed by true cormorants and sandpipers. An avian explosion impended. And the Age of Mammals as well as of birds and of flowering plants was at hand.

Mountain-making in the Cordillera in the transitional period was not confined to the raising of sedimentary ranges from the eastern side of the trough in the Laramide orogeny. Another uplift of enormous scope, still farther to the east, took place at the same time; it elevated the ancient continental basement and its veneer of younger rocks high above sea level from central Montana southward to central Arizona and central New Mexico. Great upfolds in the northern part of the region gave rise to the ranges of the Central Rocky Mountains. Others to their southeast raised the remnants of the westernmost spur of the Appalachians along with the basement, and from these the Southern Rockies were to take shape. Farther

to the south, and to the west, a block of the basement nearly five hundred miles long by five hundred broad, with a mile-deep sedimentary cover, rose *en masse*, with little deformation, to create the Colorado Plateau. By the end of the Laramide orogeny the sea had been expelled conclusively from the central lowlands—though the Gulf Coast was still far inland of where it is now. There was a long way yet to go, however, before western topography would be recognizable to modern eyes.

Not only was it without the acute relief— the vast contrast between mountaintop and gorge—of the present, but it lacked the absolute elevation as well. Before it acquired either, the whole Cordilleran region from the Great Plains westward and southward through the Colorado Plateau had to be raised bodily by a mile or more. It is uncertain exactly when and how this came about, but apparently it had taken place by the middle of the Cenozoic era, which has so far run some sixty million years. Also during the mid-Cenozoic, partly because of worldwide trends, partly because of the elevation of high ranges overlooking the Pacific, the region began to dry up. It was in the same period that geological forces were set in motion that were to undermine so drastically the Rocky Mountains south of those we call the Northern Rockies that little remains of their original form.

The burden of authority is that at some stage after the Laramide orogeny the mountains that had evolved from it became worn down until only the peaks protruded above a surface of low relief. This is analogous to the

supposed wearing down of the Appalachians to a peneplain and is hypothesized in part for the same reason—to allow the rivers a means of crossing the ranges of resistant rock through which they flow today. One school of thought holds that the leveling off took place before the great regional uplift, another that it took place after it. Whatever the facts, there is no disputing that the configuration of the ranges today is the result of erosional attack on the structures of a region that had not only been arched up by mid-Cenozoic times but has been further and extensively uplifted since then. The landscape that rises from the Great Plains on the west is to a large extent the creation of the past few million years.

Wagon trains westward bound on the Santa Fe Trail beheld at Glorieta Pass (fetching name!) a striking geological confrontation, as do motorists today on Interstate 25. On the south is the front of the plateau cut away by the Pecos, a lofty escarpment scalloped in a succession of jutting prows, somber, withdrawn, and, you would think, primordial. On the north, rising in flowing slopes, is the beginning of the Sangre de Cristo Range of the Southern Rockies and of the Cordillera.

After the southern desert comes the northern forest. And after at least a thousand miles sedimentary rock, craggy abutments of salmon-colored granite, rise beside the twisting road above Santa Fe. With pines growing from the ancient, knobby piles, the effect is Japanese. It is also like parts of New England. And farther along, as the road climbs toward Baldy Peak, which tops 12,600 feet, the slopes that

draw up and away from you could be those of the Appalachians; you do not realize your altitude—until you try to exert yourself.

The reality of what has happened where the Cordillera looms up perhaps strikes you with greatest force when you come before the majesties of the Front Range. These summits, as they come first into view, make you think of the dorsal plates of a white dragon crouched behind dark foothills. The greatest of them is Longs Peak. As the dominant feature of the range from the highway between Fort Collins and Denver, it reposes enthroned in a wilderness of giants, twin-peaked, king and queen in one. You see the procession of hoary crests half mantled in snowfields as they must have appeared to the first explorers, like a phalanx drawn up across the pathway to the hidden treasures of the Golden West.

The Garden of the Gods is being taken over by the realtors of Colorado Springs, but there, in the shadow of Pikes Peak, red sandstone walls still rise like wings of rock. Limbs are what geologists call the formations of which they are vestiges—the sides of soaring folds of stratified rock. West of Boulder, to the north, there are similar limbs, less colorful but higher, called flatirons, also listing toward the main ranges. These are the remnants of the sedimentary rocks that in the Laramide orogeny were arched up from below, layer after layer, only to be assailed by the driving rains and slowly disintegrated. For tens of millions of years it went on—until there began to nudge through the shales, limestones, and sandstones a different order of material altogether. The veteran re-

The greatest of the Front
Range Rockies is Longs Peak,
discovered by the Stephen
H. Long expedition in 1819–20.
At left, an engraving by
Samuel Seymour, a member of
the Long expedition, shows the
survey team crossing the
tablelands at the foot of the
Rockies. It was Long who
stigmatized the West as a
"great American desert" not
suited for farming, a notion
that dissuaded many Easterners
from migrating westward.

serves, the unyielding rocks of the main body, were coming up. These were not the granites of batholiths formed when the Cordillera was in the making but components of the continental basement itself, more than a billion years old. And slowly as these furnace-born metamorphic and igneous rocks arose, they rose much faster than the elements could reduce them. Now, eons later, they form the skyline of the Front Range at up to fourteen thousand feet and above from Santa Fe to the Belt Mountains east of Helena, Montana.

At the eastern foot of the range called *the* Front Range the contrast is as sharp as it could possibly be. On a stretch of the highway south from Laramie you have a red sandstone escarpment on one side of the pavement and on the other, ridges of red granite blocks weathered grey. The road to Estes Park, where the Rocky Mountain National Park begins, takes you up the narrow, twisting gorge of Big Thompson River, where you may have a good look at the rocks composing the Front Range. Where they stand naked in fresh cuts, different sorts are as colorfully juxtaposed as the rocks of the Canadian Shield—of which they are a continuation. Slate-grey schists glisten like satin in sheets ten feet across, and red and pink granites have the sparkle of tinsel when the light catches the plates of mica and huge crystals of feldspar they incorporate. At times the walls of the gorge, hundreds of feet high, threaten to close in on you. Beyond them the foothills come increasingly into view as the gorge opens out and as they gain in height, steep and pine-clad but with bare faces of grey rock, like grim-visaged

guardians of their exalted rulers beyond.

And what rulers they are! From Estes Park they stand like blocks of granite turned edge up. The rounding off that comes to lower mountains with prolonged exposure is not in evidence. Rather, the crests of their summits and ridges, above the deeply gouged flanks, have the appearance of fracture edges. As you climb the National Park's Trail Ridge Road, which zigzags up the range, the sense of their hugeness and of the fecundity of the awful incubator that hatched them grows on you; there are sixty-two more than twelve thousand feet high in the 25-by-16-mile park alone, and the Front Range is a 200-by-40-mile expanse.

"Behemoth, biggest born of earth"; Longs Peak, though 14,256 feet in height, would not quite measure up to Milton's apostrophe, but in the spectacular views of it afforded by the park's roads, it might be your visualization of Olympus. If it had to be climbed at all, one is glad that it was John Wesley Powell and his party who first assaulted it successfully, in 1868. The fragrance of Colorado blue spruce accompanies you upward from the park entrance. A Steller's jay that flies before you is like an exotic escaped from an aviary; black from its head and tall, pointed crest midway down its body, its hind parts, wings and tail, are a radiant blue. Beyond the reach of Engelmann spruce, alpine fir, and limber pine, the road goes for eleven miles in the arctic zone where trees cannot survive; dwarfed plants—which form mats called tundra—are the only plants. There are two grey, white, and black birds of the high mountain woods, stubby-

The Inside Passage, as it is called, is a sheltered waterway along the Pacific Coast from Puget Sound up into Alaska. The islands it passes among are western outriders of the Rockies. Captain Cook and Sir Francis Drake both sailed this route, as did the Alaskan gold-seekers many years later. More than a thousand miles long, the Inside Passage runs approximately the length of the Pacific Coast batholith, one of the longest igneous intrusions in the world.

billed Canada jays and Clark's nutcrackers, like small, particolored crows. The latter perch a few feet from you at the edge of chasms that fall away to metallic threads of streams in the depths below, setting the teeth on edge.

The Central and Southern Rocky Mountains have no equivalents in the Appalachian system, but between the Appalachians and those ranges of the Rocky Mountains proper that have retained their inherent structure— the Northern Rockies—the analogies are unmistakable. Visitors to Banff, in southwestern Alberta, find themselves in one of a series of long, parallel valleys separated by ridges, which together are comparable to the ridge-and-valley province of the western Appalachians. An interesting difference, however, is that here, where the climate is cold and relatively dry, it is the limestones that form the ridges and the sandstones that underlie the valleys, reversing the relationship in the Appalachians. And of course the younger Canadian ranges stand immensely higher than their analogues in the East. The stern and barren crests of the Continental Divide—the edge of steeply tilted Mississippian limestone half a mile thick—to which Banff looks up, achieve an elevation of thirteen thousand feet in Jasper National Park, to the north. In both ranges, however, cross-sections worked out by geologists show that the upthrown folds of sedimentary rock behaved in the same way, listing to the inland side, presumably as the main thrust of the uplift tilted them that way. In the Rockies as in the Appalachians, the strain on the strata was frequently more than they could take,

with the result that the upper layers were pried loose from the lower and, snapping, overrode those below. The most famous, if not the most far-reaching, of these thrust-faults is the Lewis overthrust, now part of Glacier National Park in northwestern Montana.

It is at the International Peace Park, of which Glacier is the United States portion, that probably more Americans are introduced to the Northern Rockies than anywhere else. Here the circumstances are highly peculiar.

They go back to the first sedimentation in the Rocky Mountain trough in early Paleozoic times, and beyond. One section of the trough, extending at least seven hundred miles through Montana and up into Canada, was already floored by sedimentary rocks. These rocks formed to a thickness of up to eight and a half miles in a pre-existing, inactive trough. They are known as the Belt series because of their having first been detected in the Belt Mountains. That they are now in view is the result of the height to which they were hoisted by the titanic forces brought to bear in the Laramide orogeny. This was such that, on a front hundreds of miles long, Belt rocks many thousands of feet thick slid as much as twenty miles down to the east, over the contorted, much younger, late Mesozoic rocks. The elevation they were given was also such that the kind that form the rest of the sedimentary Rockies were altogether stripped away by erosion; and mountains were hewn from the emergent Belt series by the same forces. In places the Belt rocks were cut down all the way to the underlying late Mesozoic rocks.

The Belt rocks appear to be over a billion years old and are some of the oldest above ground on the continent outside the Canadian Shield. They are today exposed over an area of some thirty thousand square miles. In the fluted peaks and great theatre walls formed by the sharp ridges of Glacier Park they are exhibited spectacularly—limestones and semi-metamorphosed shales in nearly level bands each several thousand feet thick and of varying shades. (The Belt series, surprisingly enough, were much less subject to folding than the rocks above them.) Through the uppermost limestone strata runs a 100-foot-thick sill of basalt which, before it cooled, marbleized the limestone.

Trending northwest through Canada, paralleling the coast, the sedimentary Rockies enter Alaska on the west to fan out across all the state apart from the southeastern portion. In Alaska, their major achievement is the Brooks Range in the extreme north, which divides the last of the northern forest from the treeless tundra and the ancestral lands of Indian and Eskimo. The 6,000-foot summits of the Brooks Range look north toward the Arctic Ocean across a desolate coastal plain which is more than 50 per cent in standing water—or ice.

South of the Brooks Range, and perhaps not much more inviting to most persons, stretches a plateau of hills drained chiefly by the Yukon and its tributaries. These waterways meander over floodplains on which black spruce, canoe birch, and alder crowd impenetrably together, like refugees on a waterfront. Before the advent of the airplane, rivers alone gave access to this Alaskan hinterland, whether by boat or by dogsled over ice. In winter, everything in the interior province freezes, sometimes even whiskey, and the ground over half the plateau remains frozen a foot or two below the surface all through the summer. It is this so-called permafrost that, by preventing drainage, keeps the flat tundra perpetually saturated even though the paucity of precipitation characteristic of the Arctic would turn it into a desert elsewhere. At the eastern head of the plateau are the highlands through which a once-obscure creek called the Klondike flows to join the Yukon just before the latter's crossing from Canada into Alaska. The discovery of gold in the creek in 1896 brought a stampede of eighteen thousand fortune seekers into the area, many to endure unspeakable hardships.

(While it has been stated that nearly every rock-forming process has at one place or another yielded a valuable mineral deposit, gold is generally produced where hot-water solutions at great depths deposit it in rock fissures. In this it resembles the ores of silver, copper, lead, and zinc. Indeed, it is usually found with silver or the ores of other metals and more often than not in quartz "veins"—which are actually irregular sheets that are veins in cross-section only. These sheets tend to cluster around igneous bodies, and it is thought that magma is the origin of the metal-bearing solutions that invade them. Gold rushes, like those of the Klondike, are generally touched off by the discovery of "placer" gold—flecks and nuggets of the enduring metal in stream beds into which they were washed and concentrated after the de-

composition of the gold-bearing rock.)

The forged-rock Rockies, rising on the Pacific side of the sedimentary Rockies and corresponding to the eastern Appalachians, also end, or begin, in Alaska. They are set conspicuously apart by the granite bodies they contain, of which by far the largest is the monster Coast batholith. Not only is this great granite mass long enough to connect the two mainland portions of the United States; even where it has been cut down into for seven thousand feet in the process of being carved into mountains, no sign of a bottom appears. In the Alaska panhandle and in British Columbia the plutonic Rockies do not stop at the sea. Their partially submerged outliers form the coast.

A young coast, it is without beaches. The mountains, as high as five thousand feet, rise directly out of the sea in a procession of fiords from which the sun, if not already hidden by clouds, is likely to be shut out by the towering walls. A current of equatorial water from the other side of the Pacific, flowing up alongside the Japanese archipelago and thence eastward across the Pacific's northern rim, tempers the winter on the coast of Alaska below the Aleutians. But mild temperatures are not all the ocean sends. Heavy-laden clouds in endless succession are driven upon the coastal ranges to discharge their contents upon them. From the high mountains in the northern part, where condensation takes place below the freezing point, immense rivers of snow-formed ice—glaciers—descend to the sea.

The plutonic Rockies reach their climax in the Alaska Range, and an awesome one it is.

The range occupies a position in the southern part of the state comparable to that of the Brooks Range in the north. Rising in the west from a 200-mile-long batholith, it arches eastward to an anchor in the stupendous mountain mass at the foot of the north-south border with Canada. Two super-mountains crown this highland: Mount St. Elias, rising symmetrically to an elevation of eighteen thousand feet above a creeping apron of ice seventy miles wide, became the first part of Alaska seen by white men when the Russian-employed, Danish explorer Vitus Bering sighted it from the sea in 1741; Mount Logan, standing 19,850 feet above sea level, is the highest mountain in Canada and does not miss by far being the highest in North America.

Mount Denali (also known as Mount McKinley), in the more westerly part of the range, has this distinction. Fortunate is he who has looked upon Denali's 20,320-foot-high peak broadly buttressed by crumpled, raw-edged tributary ridges, a masterwork of granite—an expanse of pink and grey granite fifteen thousand feet high forming the southern front—a spume of snow at its windy crest. And fortunate are the people who inherit this crowning eminence of the continent with a National Park three thousand square miles in extent to guard its approaches and to protect the grizzlies, moose, and wolves that make their homes in its moss-deep spruce forests, on its alpine tundra, and along its streams, the caribou that migrate through it thousands strong, and the golden eagles that soar on the winds turned upward by the mountain walls.

Atraveler in the West will be less continually surprised by its geology if he is prepared by the knowledge that in the past
seventy million years large parts of the Rocky
Mountain states and Texas and nearly all
parts of the states to the west of them have
been covered by volcanic rock. Not only has
the West in recent geologic times been one of
the most active volcanic areas in the world, but
much volcanic activity there has taken place in
the past few million years. And some, at least,
may well be in store for the future. The rise of
folded-mountain belts and the uplift and jug-
gling of crustal blocks represent mainly a rearrangement of existing continental materials.
But in the molten rock that surges up through
the crust the continent may fairly be considered to have received an increment. And
although we may think of volcanic eruptions in
terms of the effusions that buried Pompeii and
extinguished St. Pierre, the increment is of a
kind that can go far, far beyond that.

Of the accessible areas, the one that probably gives the best idea of the kind of landscape
that has predominated in the West for long periods is the lava fields preserved in the Craters
of the Moon National Monument. And as an
added recompense, a trip to the site offers the
spectacle of the Northern Rockies rising from
Idaho's Snake River plain.

As you near these craters, jumbles of lava
fragments appear, as if truckloads of broken-
up old asphalt had been dumped there. This is
lava of a kind known as *aa* (a two-syllable Hawaiian word). In eruptions it tumbles forward
in masses of jagged lumps, viscously molten in-

Volcanic debris creates a no man's land in Lassen Volcanic National Park, California.

side. There are miles of it within and around
the monument, along with solidified rivers,
mounds, and slumps of *pahoehoe* (also Hawaiian, of five syllables). This type of lava, being
much more fluid, can flow for long distances,
and when it hardens it does so in ropy or bil-
lowy forms, like congealed tar, or in the semblance of gigantic, crusted cow pats. Where the
surface of a flow of pahoehoe hardens while the
mass within is still moving, a hollow cylinder
may be left behind; some in the Craters Monument are as big as houses or vehicular tunnels.
Above the lava fields, following a rift in the
earth, rises a line of volcanic cones. Those of
volcanic grit, so-called cinder cones, resemble
hills of pulverized coal on railroad sidings, but
are mammoth. Other cones are of the spatter
type, collared by blobs of lava that have fallen
molten around their craters—the same kind
that, hurled higher into the air, harden before
striking the earth as spindle-shaped "bombs."
Lava was issuing from fissures here as recently
as sixteen hundred years ago, though by its appearance it could be only days old.

The Snake River, whose waters by the time
they reach the Pacific could perhaps tell more
about lava rock than those of any other river in
the world, rises in the high tableland of Yellowstone Park, in the western part of the Absaroka Range. This is one of the great lava highlands on the frontier of the volcanic West.
Driving up the Wind River valley to the
park's south entrance, you will know that you
have arrived at the frontier when the highway
climbs between two geological edifices that
bring to mind Shakespeare's "fortress built by

nature for herself." One is a 10,000-foot butte
of enormous minars called Lava Mountain.
The other is called the Palisades but is actually
several palisades stacked to a towering height.
Both are of dark mauve, stratified volcanic
rock. Such rock is everywhere in the park.
Most notably it forms the canyon in which the
Yellowstone River plunges first over one hundred feet, then over three hundred. In most
lights it is a greyish brown, about the color of
the elk that browse by the score on the open
flats. In their last active period, the volcanoes
that created these highlands disgorged more
than six hundred cubic miles of rhyolite—the
fine-grained, volcanic form of granite. Two-
thirds of it issued as torrents of ash or glassy
grit, which was still so hot on settling it was
fused into rock. Valleys and ridges alike were
buried in layers of this welded tuff, as it is
called, along with sheets of lavas. The present
mountains appeared with the carving up of
the plateaus that grew from the eruptions.

The history of the Absarokas was also that
of the lofty San Juans of southern Colorado
and of the Jemez Mountains of northern New
Mexico. In the latter case, the eruption of lava
from a super-volcano sufficient to create fifty
cubic miles of welded tuff left a chasm beneath
the cone into which a circular block of the
earth's crust over ten miles wide dropped several thousand feet. This kind of collapse, leaving a crater of colossal size, termed a caldera, is
typical of major volcanic eruptions, but the
Valles Caldera is one of the world's largest.
And its distinction does not stop there. Subsequent upwellings of lava beneath it were such

as to arch its floor up to a greater height than ever and spawn fifteen new volcanoes on its perimeter. The Geological Survey tells us, moreover, that tens of thousands of cubic miles of welded rhyolitic tuffs are known in Nevada (where perhaps half the ranges show on the geologic map as volcanic rock) and great quantities are also found in two other areas: the Big Bend region of Texas and the mountainous region saddling the border between Arizona and New Mexico below the Colorado Plateau.

These six regions comprise all but one of the major volcanic fields outside the supreme volcanic province of the Northwest. The seventh is centered along a line of former volcanoes fifty or sixty miles south of the Grand Canyon. Of these, the greatest and most beautiful is *Nuvatukia Ovi*—"The Place of Snow on the Very Top" of the Hopis—which rises abruptly north of Flagstaff. Called the San Francisco Peaks by Europeans, it must once have stood well over fifteen thousand feet high and have resembled Fuji, but erosion has removed an estimated three thousand feet from the top. As you see it now from the Grand Canyon, it has the form of a broad, jagged crater. Doubtless it was the leading contributor to the lava that flooded the plains for fifty miles around it and its neighbors during a period from about a million years ago until the time the Vikings appeared off our coast.

That Yellowstone was made a National Park in 1872 (and a precedent set for the designation of more than thirty others) was probably owing primarily to the incomparable display it makes of thermal phenomena. In the thick of it you have steam rising all around you. Some is roaring like a locomotive. Red mud is plopping up in boiling pits, and a fountain of more dilute red mud is shooting up several feet. Superheated vapor is hissing up as from a rent in a radiator. Sulphurous yellow waters are bubbling in a caldron in the rocks and emitting asphyxiating fumes. Hot streams are pouring down flights of terraced pools formed of the travertine they have deposited. (A form of calcium carbonate, like stalactites and stalagmites, travertine is one of the building materials most coveted in the world.) Scalding water is standing in turquoise pools. And geysers are blowing—the greatest geysers in the world, with Old Faithful sending its plume fifteen stories high. The explanation is that not very far below the surface lies a mass of still sizzling-hot lava rock with which underground streams are coming in contact. The consequences could scarcely be more theatrical if they were of human contrivance. The manifestations at Yellowstone are held to be characteristic of a receding volcanism, but apparently one should not necessarily count on this. The earthquake that brought part of Mount Jackson crashing down on August 17, 1959, was hardly a guarantee of quiescence.

The volcanic region comprising the southwestern quarter of Washington, nearly all Oregon, and western and southern Idaho is the largest in North America apart from the area which extends more than a thousand miles down through Mexico in the Sierra Madre Occidental. What crustal disturbances caused the upwellings of lava that took place here

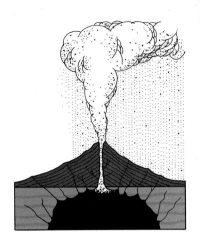

The sequence at right depicts the transformation of Oregon's Mount Mazama into Crater Lake. In a series of catastrophic events that occurred about six thousand years ago, the volcanic mountain spewed a tremendous volume of lava. Inside the volcano a great mass of magma was withdrawing into the earth. As a result a huge cavity was created, into which the top of the mountain collapsed. Rain and melted snow have since half-filled the 4,000-foot-deep chamber.

throughout the Cenozoic era are unknown.

The flow seems at least to have begun in an embrasure of the original range, where, having turned southeast from the Vancouver region to western Idaho (the location of the Idaho batholith), it bent back almost due west, touching today's coast again in the Klamath Mountains on the Oregon-California border. In early Cenozoic times, when the initial outpourings of lava apparently took place, thousands of feet of sediments were being laid down on a coastal plain and on the ocean bottom beyond it in a zone across the opening of the embrasure, between the Vancouver area and the Klamaths. While these were accumulating, basaltic lava spread out over them in successive flows, mostly under water and totaling as much as forty thousand cubic miles. Much later the solidified sedimentary strata and the interbedded lavas were folded, metamorphosed, and uplifted to form the Coast Ranges of Washington and Oregon. For most of its extent the range is not very imposing. Still, it may represent the vanguard of the continent's advance, built upon oceanic crust (the dramatic headlands it puts out to sea go with the role), and the stature it may achieve in the future is unknowable.

By mid-Cenozoic times, thirty million years ago, during the period when the major parts of the Cordillera were probably raised to their present heights, the source of volcanic upwelling had shifted eastward. In the course of more millions of years, molten basalt gushed up in successive floods to cover an area of one hundred thousand square miles, inland of the site of the future Coast Ranges. From the way it

spread, it must have been as fluid as water, and hence very hot. The plateau built up by these incandescent tides out of the inferno—the Columbia Plateau—replaced a considerable section of the Rocky Mountains, which presumably foundered as the earth's crust sank beneath them. Much later, in the past million years, renewed upwellings still farther east filled what are now the Snake River plains.

Any water reaching the sea from the Columbia Plateau reaches it via the Columbia River, to which the Snake is a major tributary. These together, in fact, drain almost all Washington, Oregon, and Idaho. In the process, they have cut gorges that show how deep the lava beds go. Flowing westward from Wyoming across Idaho, and tumbling over great cataracts, the Snake is in a canyon most of the way. Turning north to form the border with Oregon, it pours through Hells Canyon, which it has cleaved a mile deep through volcanic rocks that go back to the beginning of Mesozoic times, or beyond; clearly, volcanism did not begin here with the Cenozoic flows. Where it turns west into Washington, the Snake is only 740 feet above sea level and has the entire width of the Columbia Plateau to cross. More significantly, it has between it and the sea the barrier of the Cascade Range, many thousands of feet high. This arises on the other side of the plateau, beyond the Snake's junction with the Columbia, which comes down brimming with snowmelt from the Northern Rockies. The combined streams have necessarily dug themselves ever lower in the plateau as they approach the barrier. How can they ever have breached it? Many geologists

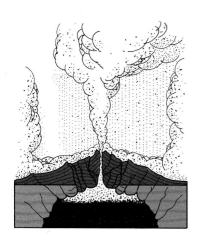  

consider it a case of an antecedent stream, so-called, a river that continued cutting a pre-existing bed as the land rose beneath it. However it was achieved, the breakthrough has left a gorge five thousand feet deep.

The Cascade Range represents another chapter in the volcanic history of the Northwest, one midway between the Coast Ranges and the Columbia Plateau and overlapping both. But the estimated twenty-five thousand cubic miles of lava that built the Cascades differed from that which overflowed through fissures to the west and east. The Cascade lavas were mostly andesite, a form intermediate chemically between basalt and rhyolite, a form of granite. And in large part they were erupted explosively, as solid lava fragments. Instead of spreading out far and thin, they built up into highlands like the Absaroka and San Juan ranges, but longer. And, like those, they were hewn into mountains by erosion.

The Cascades proper—those composed of the lavas erupted in the middle periods of the Cenozoic, from about forty to fifteen million years ago—are not particularly spectacular. The Cascades that arise in northern Washington above Stevens Pass, through which U.S. Highway 2 runs, are awesome. For one thing, it is said that their heights give rise to about half the roughly one thousand glaciers in the forty-eight states. Composed in large part of granitic rocks (including the continent's youngest), they are described by their devotees as the finest alpine country in the United States.

The supreme feature of the Cascades is the irregular line of young volcanic peaks that crown the range from near the Canadian border into California. The peaks are the work of the last million years, and five of the dozen are considered still active though dormant, with a problematical future. Like all great conical volcanoes, they were built up of layers of both molten lava and solid lava fragments: volcanic ash, grit, pumice, and rocks. And the material was still mostly the grey andesite. Volcanoes of this type in their capes of snow—ice queens, true solitaires among mountains—appear to stand outside the earthbound order of things. Seeing Mount Shasta in northern California rising to 14,162 feet, you almost feel that if you turned away you might look back to find her gone. And nothing that is beautiful was ever rendered less so by being dangerous. One can never be sure of any of these great cone volcanoes. Moreover, on the summits of even the most peaceful, conditions are likely to be merciless most of the time. In the winter of 1955-56, eighty feet of snow fell at a station on the southern slope of Mount Rainier. But if Rainier threatens the lives of untimely visitors with her blizzards, she has succored more than one in her steam caves. Her dome of raw rock protruding through sagging, ever-replenished ice fields that reach far down through the ravines, is peaked at 14,410 feet, making her virtually as tall as the tallest mountain in the forty-eight states.

The greatest eruption in the Cascades, and possibly even in the world, within the memory of man was that of Mount Mazama in Oregon. An event of around six thousand years ago but one apparently still recalled in Indian lore, it

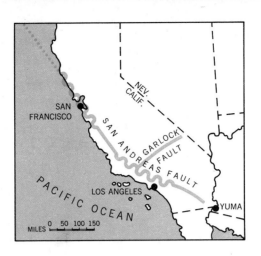

The disastrous San Francisco earthquake of 1906 was caused by a crustal shifting of up to twenty-one feet along the San Andreas fault (shown at right with the Garlock fault branching to the east). An estimated annual shifting of two inches along the western side of the fault is gradually moving the crust there to the north. Theoretically, in about eleven million years this could make San Francisco and Los Angeles twin cities.

must have rivaled or exceeded the most devastating eruption of historic times: that in 1883 of Krakatoa. So much lava was discharged from Mazama as ash and pumice that seventeen cubic miles of the 12,000-foot mountain collapsed into the hole that was left. The caldera thus created is now filled by a lake six miles across and nearly two thousand feet deep surrounded by cliffs of up to two thousand feet high. Although Crater Lake is at an elevation noted for its severe winters, it never freezes. Though without an outlet, it is not salty. And its waters are of a blue probably unmatched in intensity by any others anywhere.

The volcanoes of the Cascades are part of the circum-Pacific "ring of fire," one of two sectors north of Central America. The other follows the 2,000-mile-long arc of the Alaskan Peninsula and the Aleutian Islands. Strung out through the arc are no less than forty volcanoes that have been active in historic times, in addition to an equal number now extinct. Some are superb in form and in a less remote region would be famous. In a less remote region, however, one of them, which erupted in 1912, might have produced one of the great disasters of recorded times. As it was, preliminary tremors sent the few inhabitants of the area to safety. The eruption was from the foot of Mount Katmai, at the base of the peninsula. With a roar heard 750 miles away in Juneau, it expelled about two cubic miles of white-hot ash and pumice, an avalanche of which—called "rivers of sand" by those who came later—flowed for fifteen miles down an adjacent valley, filling it to a depth of four hundred feet.

This was named the Valley of Ten Thousand Smokes, in which even today some steam and vapors are being emitted from a few vents. Kodiak Island, ninety miles to the east, was covered by a foot of ash. Dust from the explosion overspread the world, still present in snow-cores taken in the Arctic and Antarctic.

One of the earliest impressions any European had of the Cordillera was of the Santa Lucia Range, which forms the coast for a hundred miles south of Monterey Bay—the so-called Big Sur coast. Sailing by here in 1542, Juan Rodriguez Cabrillo wrote: "All the coast passed this day is very bold; there is a great swell and the land is very high. There are mountains which seem to reach the heavens, and the sea beats on them; sailing along close to land, it appears as if they would fall on the ships." The Coast Ranges of California, like those of Oregon and Washington, attain a height of about eight thousand feet at their northern extremity but elsewhere are considerably lower. They are folded-mountain belts as young as any in the world. Those in California, however, seem to go back to older events than those in the north. And they confront geology with a mystery over which brains have been wracked for many years.

Basically, these ranges consist of sedimentary rocks of the kind normally found in the outer side of sedimentary troughs, piled up along the shore in Mesozoic times and much folded, deformed, and locally metamorphosed at the end of that period. Later, these Franciscan rocks, as they are termed, were raised in blocks. Greatly eroded, they form the larger

97

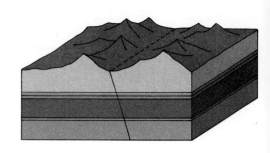

parts of the California Coast Ranges. The peculiar circumstance is that they are divided into two sections by a kind of corridor which extends north-northwest from the Transverse Ranges (the San Gabriel and San Bernardino mountains) to reach the coast at Monterey Bay, seventy-five miles south of San Francisco. In this corridor, the rocks are plutonic. There is thus a sandwich. There are Franciscan rocks on the west in the Santa Lucia Mountains and Santa Catalina Island, and there are many more on the east and north. But between them, sharply divided from them, there is this thick slice of plutonic rocks which seems to have no relationship to them. Where did it come from?

One feature to notice is that the corridor is bounded on the east by a 600-mile-long rent in the earth's crust known as the San Andreas fault. A clean rupture at least twenty miles deep, the fault extends from the Gulf of California northwest along the southern side of the San Bernardino Mountains and northern side of the San Gabriel Mountains and then north-northwest past San Francisco and through the bases of Point Reyes and Point Arena out across the ocean floor. In 1857 there had been a severe earthquake along the fault in the San Gabriel Mountains, but no repetition had been looked for and not much thought was given to the San Andreas fault until five o'clock in the morning of April 18, 1906. At that hour, disaster struck San Francisco, one that was to leave more than five hundred dead and twenty-eight thousand buildings destroyed. While an earthquake was the primary cause, most of the property damage was caused by a fire that

swept the city and could not be brought under control for three days, owing to the peculiar nature of the earth movement responsible for the quake. Almost two hundred miles of the earth's crust alongside the San Andreas fault had given a sudden lurch, the lurch at its maximum having carried it twenty-one feet. (It might be more accurate to say that the crust on both sides had lurched, in opposite directions.) Every watermain crossing the zone of fracture had been severed and offset—draining the reservoirs—as had roads, fences, streams, and everything else that crossed it.

One effect of San Francisco's misfortune was, not unnaturally, to stimulate much greater interest in the fault responsible. Thus it has been found that the older the terrain features severed by the fault the farther apart the two sides have been carried. Existing streams have been offset by as much as half a mile. Features dating back a million years have been offset about fifteen miles. Estimates of total displacement along the fault since its start perhaps 100 million years ago run as high as 350 miles. The crust on the west is moving north with respect to the crust on the east, leading to the saying that Los Angeles, which is on the west, is moving closer to San Francisco, which is on the east. Along one segment of the fault movement may proceed gradually, with frequent small shocks, where in another there may be severe earthquakes occurring in groups at intervals of between ten and twenty years. Many believe that the serious trouble is in store when rocks on one side of the fault lock with those on the other. According to this interpretation, strains

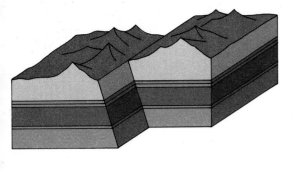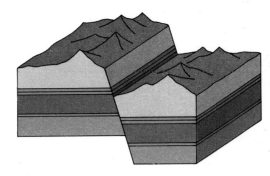

then build up until they are sufficient to overcome the impediment, at which time they give the effect of a bowstring being released.

Actually, the San Andreas fault is only the most prominent among a series of faults in western and southern California. Most of these parallel it or trend off from it, but one important one, the Garlock fault, branches off eastward along the lower edge of the Sierra Nevada; the Mohave Desert is a wedge between the Sierra and Garlock faults on the northern side and the San Andreas fault and Transverse Ranges on the southern. This brings up another odd feature of the Coast Ranges, analogous to the first. Another corridor of plutonic rocks cuts across their southern terminus, this one incorporating the Transverse Ranges and running due west out to sea to encompass Santa Clara, Santa Rosa, and the other Channel Islands west of Los Angeles.

One account for these exceedingly troublesome salients of plutonic rock is given by Philip G. King, of the U.S. Geological Survey, who offers a daring hypothesis. The hypothesis proposes that the rocks of the two salients once were part of the emerging forged-rock Rocky Mountain belt, which at that time would have formed the coast of California. The Franciscan rocks would have bordered it, lying on the continental slope or on the oceanic crust. The two long segments of plutonic rock, it is suggested, were sliced from the parent body by the movement of the earth's crust along the great faults. The theory states that one, together with the adjacent Franciscan rocks, was carried north along the San Andreas fault while the other, consisting of a whole section of the nascent Rocky Mountain belt, was swiveled and strung out into the sea by the east-west faults, leaving the Transverse Ranges like an open butterfly valve between the Sierra and the Peninsula ranges. If such was the case, rocks from the Los Angeles area, going north, have already passed San Francisco to form Point Reyes and Point Arena, just as the other set has moved as much as one hundred miles offshore.

For the rest, developments along the coast have proceeded more conventionally with the piling up of sediments on the older rocks in Cenozoic times and with their folding and uplift. The shaping of the Coast Ranges' main formation seems to have taken place some twenty million years ago and their raising as recently as the mid-Pleistocene, only half a million years back. Even in the past million years, sediments a mile thick have been deposited in some parts of the range, formed into rock, and folded in the mountain-making process. Terraces in the ranges above the Pacific show how platforms cut by waves in the sea cliffs have been progressively raised, in witness of the ranges' continuing growth, which they indicate has occurred locally in spurts. In Oregon, one of these terraces stands fifteen hundred feet above the sea. The seismograph, moreover, testifies that all is still far from quiet below. That more earthquakes are in prospect along the fault is likely. Whatever it may signify, San Francisco has experienced no tremor of importance since the disaster of 1906 (except for a lesser shock in 1957), while the last in the Los Angeles area was the quake of 1857.

THE BLOCK FORMATIONS OF THE CORDILLERA

Medicine Bow, Wyoming, the sign says. Pop. 392. The flat little town is dusty and dreary, and all around are only bleak and scrubby plains. Small wonder the American cowboy sang to keep his spirits up.

Medicine Bow is in a basin between high range, of the Southern Rockies, but only some very low ridges in the south lift the horizon. It is astonishing to find at Medicine Bow that you are 6,653 feet above sea level. You could well be less than a hundred. Following the Wind River down the southwestern edge of the Bighorn Basin, you see no sign of the ranges for which the country around you is famous.

What you do see are cliffs—cliffs of alternating levels of brick- and buff-colored sandstone; of red sandstone rising in walls straight up from the highway; of lavender-colored strata with sandy, pea-green topping; of resistant sandstone interspersed with weaker shales, which in turn have been hollowed out to give the structure the appearance of weird apartment houses. What has happened is that enormous valleys, inherently deep and V-shaped (one supposes), have been filled with sediments which, relithified, have themselves been gashed deep and wide by renewed erosion. To an Easterner the resultant scenery, characteristic of the arid West, is so exotic he can scarcely credit his being in a part of the world that sends Congressmen to Washington. And he seldom expects what turns up next—for example, Crowheart Butte, which towers all by itself above the Wind River plain. Crowheart Butte (so named when a Shoshoni chief in 1866 wardanced there with a crow's heart on his lance)

This water-carved cathedral of rock is now submerged behind Glen Canyon Dam.

This exquisitely rendered panorama of the Grand Canyon was drawn by William Henry Holmes, an artist who served several of the Government's geologic surveys of the West. The drawing was first published in 1882, in Clarence Dutton's Tertiary History of the Grand Cañon District. *Dutton opposed the "severe ascetic style" so common to scientific books; his lively prose and Holmes' magnificent art made the book a classic.*

stands seven hundred feet high, giving a staggering, if grossly inadequate, idea of the volume of detritus laid down in the basin and subsequently washed away. Such detritus not only filled the basins, it was spread eastward by slackening streams down the slope the land had been given by the uplift of the Cordillera. The surface of the Great Plains, which stands a mile high at the foot of the Front Range, consists for the most part of these deposits—that is, those of the last twenty million years.

A geologist upon whom the vast transport of sediments in the West early made an impression was Captain Clarence E. Dutton of the Powell Survey. Determining that rock strata between one and two miles in thickness had been stripped from a great plateau in Utah, he speculated upon the effect such vast shifting of material would have on the earth's crust. If the crust sagged under the weight of enormous deposits, as James Hall had convincingly argued, would it not rise when freed of them? Finding it incredible that the mountains of the region had ever stood from eight to ten miles high, as they would "if the matter removed from them could be replaced," he argued that they had only "been pushed upward as fast as they were degraded . . . by erosion." Reasoning that the earth would have "a tendency to bulge where the lighter matter had accumulated and a tendency to sag where the denser matter existed," he declared that "for this condition of equilibrium . . . to which gravitation tends to reduce a planetary body . . . I propose the name of isostasy." Thus, in a talk to the Philosophical Society of Washington in 1889, was a

name given to a key concept of geology.

Dutton, a native of Connecticut, Class of 1860 at Yale, wrote one of his two major works on the Grand Canyon; his sensitive description, accompanied by William Henry Holmes' masterly drawings, helped to awaken the nation to its "sublime" character, as he called it.

A tortuous, gaping incision in the western part of the Colorado Plateau over two hundred miles long, four to eighteen miles wide, and a mile deep, with convoluted sides so steep as to be almost everywhere unscalable, the Grand Canyon tells more than could possibly otherwise be known about that block of the earth's crust, almost the size of Texas, which was originally uplifted along with the Central and Southern Rockies in the late Mesozoic era. "Nowhere else on earth," as Joseph Wood Krutch remarks, is there "a valley or canyon at once so deep, so long and so closely hemmed in by its walls." And perhaps nowhere else is there a landform that stirs such an awareness of the scale on which the earth's raw materials are distributed and redistributed—indeed, of the meaning of geology.

That there could be such an exhibition required more than the raising of the continental basement and its superincumbent strata in the Colorado Plateau. If the Colorado River was to file its way deep into the basement rocks as it has done, it required the further arching of the mass to raise a portion even higher. And that was accomplished in the Kaibab uplift, a bulge about one hundred miles long by twenty-five wide. In the process, the upper strata to a thickness of thousands of feet have been worn

off. It is as if a stack of pancakes (which sedimentary strata seem inevitably to suggest) had been arched up so as to come just within reach of hungry fingers stretched down from above. The stripping away of the convex layers has carried all the way down to one of resistant, late Paleozoic limestone. Kaibab limestone, as it is called, now forms the surface of the plateau for which it is named. It stands at seven thousand feet above sea level along the south rim of the Grand Canyon and at eight thousand feet along the north rim, whence, after rising another thousand feet farther north, it slopes downward to pass beneath the edge of the next younger stratum at half the elevation in southern Utah.

Since the Colorado River could scarcely have flowed up over the Kaibab Plateau in preparation for cutting its way through, the question of how it has accomplished this feat has long been pondered. John Wesley Powell, combating the tenacious view that rivers took their courses from cracks in the earth left by convulsive disorders, proposed the idea of "antecedent" streams. His theory was that rivers that cut through highlands are simply following the course they had before the highlands were raised, having continuously cut their beds lower as the uplift took place, the one process keeping pace with the other. For some years this theory was held to explain the Grand Canyon. Obstacles came to light, however, and the view prevailing today seems to be that this is a case of "headwaters erosion." If the view is correct, there were two Colorado Rivers when the plateau was raised. There was the present upper Colorado, which flowed down the eastern side of the plateau and thence to the Gulf of Mexico, probably through the Rio Grande; and there was the present lower Colorado, which arose on the western side of the plateau and followed about the same course it does today to the Gulf of California. The two became joined (it is hypothesized) when the latter, nourished by rains falling on the high, western slopes, ate its way back through the plateau to capture the waters of the former—a theory that would account for the abrupt turn from southeast to west the Colorado now makes by passing through a U-bend in the floor of the Grand Canyon.

The plain leading to the canyon from the south is featureless except for a low, lonely mountain standing head and shoulders above it. Protected by a cap of conglomerate sandstone, Red Butte is all that remains of the Mesozoic strata that once covered the plateau to immense depths.

With all the stunning photographs there are of the canyon two things about it are yet likely to surprise you when you first look into it. One is the breadth of the conifer-speckled shelf, called the Tonto Platform, far down in the abyss, above the narrow, inner gorge. The other is the insignificance of the river at the bottom of the gorge, of which only a very short segment at best is likely to be visible. You feel you could jump over it. Though you are told it is three hundred feet wide, you can hardly conceive how it could have cut the canyon, even with the help of all the rains that have so deeply gullied the canyon's flanks. The Colorado is

The view from the rim of the Grand Canyon (far left), considered by many the most awesome spectacle on earth, reveals the steep, giant steps that have resulted from the weathering of rocks of varying resistance over millions of years. The layers (immediately below) are alternating bands of limestone, sandstone, and shale, except in the deepest part of the canyon, where the rocks are Precambrian— primarily schist but frequently granite (bottom picture). A mile below the rim the Colorado River is still cutting away, though more slowly than it once did, for the Precambrian rock is hard, and Glen Canyon Dam, upstream, has slackened the river's flow. The geologically recent cuts (below, right) are steep and narrow, but in time the walls will disintegrate, as the upper walls have done. Eons hence, the Grand Canyon may again be what it was ten million years ago: a flat plain.

It is not known for certain who sketched this profile of the geologic findings of Powell's second Colorado River expedition (1871–72). But assuredly it was Powell himself who provided the earliest insights into the complicated history of that region of the West. Though Powell had little interest in stratigraphy, he was fascinated by geologic processes— especially erosion, the carver of the great canyons along the Colorado River he explored.

characteristically mud-colored; normally it carries a million tons of silt daily through the canyon. It has given promise of filling Lake Mead with sand and mud up to the top of Boulder Dam in a century. But much of its load is now being entrapped upstream in Lake Powell, behind Glen Canyon Dam, and except when the Little Colorado is bringing in silt from rains in the Painted Desert, the river flows through Grand Canyon a beautiful lime green.

The river is walled by the dark schists of the continental basement. The remains of mountains long ago planed down to their bases, the chaotic rocks of the inner gorge are at least 1,350 million years old; that has been found to be the age of the granite that has cut through them, forming dikes visible even from the rim. Above the inner gorge, the canyon consists of an intricately rain-slashed stack of vertical walls, each wall stepped back from the one below and generally separated from it by a slope. The stack in some places ascends almost straight up from the river; in others it is staggered so far back that the rim stands ten miles from the river. Each wall and each slope represent different depositional epochs, beginning with a 250-foot-thick layer of Precambrian sandstone resting on the basement schists and forming the foundation of the Tonto Platform. Together they give a good idea of the contents of the inland side of the prenatal Rocky Mountain trough, for they were laid down on its eastern margin where, it should be noted, the sediments were thinning out toward the interior. Together, also, they embrace the entire Paleozoic era, though with two hiatuses of tens

of millions of years when the terrain stood high enough so that deposition ceased and may have been succeeded by erosion.

Statistics tell you that the dark, seemingly small inner gorge matches the height of the Empire State Building. The Redwall, a prominent cliff banding the canyon about halfway up, is as high as the Washington Monument. (Of Mississippian limestone, it is a natural blue-grey but has been stained by the iron oxides from the red sandstone and shale above it.) The belt of limestone at the top, pale buff to pale grey, is equally high, and the wall of almost white sandstone beneath it is as high as a thirty-story building.

But you cannot truly comprehend the scale of the Grand Canyon. This makes somewhat mystifying the effect it has on you—and there must be many who would agree that no other visual experience the continent affords has a profounder one. Beforehand, you cannot believe the reality will live up to what you have been told to expect. And yet it does. Krutch speaks of the sense of vast emptiness and the absolute solitude to which the canyon conduces even in the near presence of hordes of men. In truth, it engulfs you in both. Everyone has known the spell of an evening hush upon a valley. The utter repose and silence, the utter immobility of this tremendous chasm is like that hush, but as an ocean to a lake.

One would suppose that anybody who comes here must feel that the canyon has a special meaning for him, to be divined in exploration of the layered rocks that are five thousand feet from top to bottom and a billion years in the

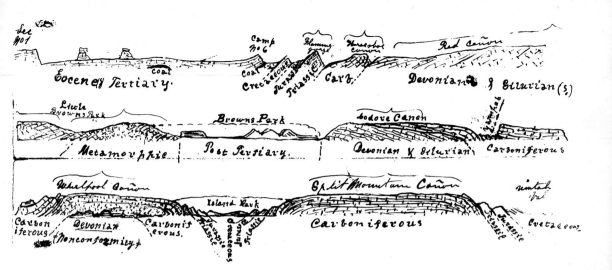

accumulation. For an awful and eerie significance seems attached to the phenomenon of the canyon, such as might bespeak the direct intervention of a Creator. The projections of limestone above the sheer drops, sculptured in the suggestion of immense gargoyles, call up images of impassive earth-genies obedient to a supreme summons to stand revealed in this one place. You hear the rolling croak of a raven somewhere, and one will rise from the depths of the canyon on an updraft, or sail along the rim. The great stone profiles gaze enigmatically off across the canyon, blue in the heat of noon in its depths where the black schists have been disinterred from an ancient oblivion. Perhaps the ultimate feeling the canyon instills is that time is like space, and that which has been lived through does not cease to exist, any more than a place one has traveled through vanishes because one has left it behind.

One would like to believe that such is the case—and not least in the Petrified Forest. This is at the end of the Painted Desert, which curves from the eastern side of the Kaibab Plateau for 170 miles south and east. There, in parts of the bottomlands, sections of the brown, stony logs lie around like drums, some as large as three feet in diameter. At Blue Mesa you can see how they are exhumed. Some protrude from the rim of the mesa while others down the slope are perched on pedestals of the grey clay, which they have shielded from erosion. But eventually the rainwash does its work and down they come. Pine-like trees once growing on slopes above swamps akin to those of the eastern coal basins, they were swept downstream and buried periodically under clay and sand, as the coal forests were, and under volcanic grit. Their decay was inhibited by lack of oxygen; water charged with silica seeped through their pores. In some cases it filled them with quartz and left the wood preserved. In most, it replaced the organic matter with minerals, so that what was wood became agate and jasper.

Of those vast, teeming floodplains of 180 to 200 million years ago, some fossils and the petrified tree trunks, cast up in the wastes of the Little Colorado's badlands, are all that remain. All else is gone, buried under continental, then marine, silts. Thus are whole worlds—as seemingly secure as our own for millions of years, the standard for what is natural and normal—extinguished and, usually with no jeweled images of corpses, resurrected through an off chance, to convey what they had been.

Their dissolution retarded by their capping of sandstone blocks fit for a Stonehenge, the splayed mounds and mesas of the Painted Desert are vertically cut with grooves like the wrinkles in a crone's face and banded in brick-red, grey, and mauve. They are composed of the Mesozoic deposits of which the Kaibab Plateau has been denuded. On the other side of the plateau, if you proceed into Utah, you recover the Mesozoic deposits chapter by chapter, in a series of escarpments. Oddly, as you progress, climbing over one after another, you are also gradually descending. These are the edges of the humped pancakes, as far as the hungry fingers have been able to strip them back. Then there are the Chocolate Cliffs, of an early Mesozoic conglomerate; the Vermilion Cliffs, of early-middle Mesozoic sandstone formed of desert dunes; the White Cliffs, of mid-Mesozoic sandstone of similar origin; and the Gray Cliffs, of late Mesozoic sandstones and shales. (If these sound like the obstacles the hero of a fairy tale must surmount, it is nonetheless how they are described in sober geologic studies.)

In Zion Canyon, one hundred miles northwest of Grand Canyon, the Virgin River has cut a chasm through the rocks that form the Vermilion and White cliffs. The lower two thousand feet of the walls are of the red sandstone, the upper of the white. And these are in truth walls, perpendicular cliffs, with Great White Throne rising 2,400 feet above the flat canyon bottom and West Temple rising 3,800 feet. Rainbow Bridge, soaring thirty stories high in southeastern Utah, and now reached by the waters of Lake Powell, is of the same red sandstone, as are the 500-foot canyon walls on either side of it.

On the highest plateaus, above the Gray Cliffs, there is even another step—the Pink Cliffs, of early Cenozoic limestones and sandstones, probably formed in inland seas and lakes. In Bryce Canyon, forty miles east of Zion, these uplifted beds are displayed in horizontally grooved walls, towers, and pinnacles that resemble cathedrals and myriad crowded minarets, or attenuated, giant chessmen, variously pink-stained or of the natural creamy color of the limestone. Not so much a canyon as the edge of a plateau deeply eaten out by flowing water and incised by the freezing and

thawing of melted snow, the rock formations of Bryce are considered by many the most beautiful on the continent. But wherever streams run on the Colorado Plateau there are cliffs and canyons, towering mesas, buttes, spires, natural archways—the monumental statuary of imposing giants in lost worlds.

In holding that the earth owes its physiognomy to cataclysmic events of stupefying violence, the old-time geologists may have erred; they did err in their conception of the tempo of the events and in assigning them to a closed chapter of history. But they were not far off the mark in their estimate of the intensity of the convulsions themselves. A speeding up of geological change to compress millions of years into minutes would produce spectacles satisfying even our forefathers' notions of what was worthy of a Deity aroused to full exercise of His omnipotence. If we visualize the frozen surface of a river ridged with windrows of melted and refrozen snow and then imagine such turbulence set up in the river as would break the ice into long cakes, dropping some to a lower level and raising others on a steep slant, then enlarge the scale several thousandfold, we shall have a picture of catastrophism on a par with the visions of the past and also a fair idea of what befell the earth's crust from the Northern Rockies well into Mexico in the past ten million years.

What kind of turbulence there was is not known—and the word is hardly suitable for processes as stately as those must have been, barring such occasional sudden slippages along the faults as may jar cities down today. It is

speculated, however, that the earth's crust was stretched laterally in the Basin and Range Province, just as it was compressed laterally to produce the mountain chains on either side of it. The manner in which the Rocky Mountains, which form a compact bundle of ranges in Canada, bulge out sideways in the United States before narrowing again in Mexico tempts one to relate their doing so with the stretching out of the crust encompassed by them—if, indeed, it *was* stretched out.

Whatever the mechanism responsible, fault-block mountains predominate throughout the so-called Basin and Range Province. (This occupies the lower portion of a vast region of plains and tablelands interspersed with abrupt features of high relief that spreads from southeastern Washington and southern Idaho to southeastern California and thence eastward below the rim of the Colorado Plateau across southern Arizona and New Mexico to western Texas and down into Mexico.) And even the Colorado Plateau has been affected by the crustal breakup (so much so that in the west it falls off down several widely separated steps, each formed by the down-drop of the eastern edge of a long block of the crust). Descending the last of the steps, a rugged escarpment, you pass between a jumble of mountains on the south with a saw-toothed ridgeline—the Aquarius Mountains—and on the north a very long, jagged range—the Grand Wash Cliffs; these ranges begin the fault-block mountains.

The forces that reshuffled this huge, central Cordilleran region were no respecters of existing structures. With the fracturing of the crust into blocks, along lines that took a generally north-south direction, whatever made up the blocks was either dropped to form basins or rift valleys (the Rio Grande flows through such a valley in New Mexico) or thrust up, more often than not on a sharp tilt. Some of the blocks are of folded strata of the kind that compose the sedimentary Rockies. Of such a block are the Grand Tetons, which rise just south of Yellowstone Park, though in their case most of the sedimentary strata have worn off to expose a core of uplifted basement rocks. Another example is the Wasatch Mountains below them, which divide Utah in two and face west, across the Basin and Range Province toward the Sierra Nevada. (By "face" is meant the face of the fracture that has been uplifted as the steep side of a fault-block mountain, as opposed to the much more gradual slope of the top of the block.) The Sierra Nevada, which also look out across the province, are of rocks such as form the plutonic Rockies—folded strata (mostly Paleozoic) and, above all, solid granite. They form the longest and most formidable mountain barrier in the United States and probably the world's largest fault-block mountain. Presumably all three ranges were parts of conventional folded-mountain belts before the great fragmentation and *bouleversement*, but their structures now bear little relationship to what they would have been then. In the north, on the eastern edge of the Great Sandy Desert of Oregon, you encounter a fault-block of wholly different composition. Abert Rim, a monstrous mesa topped by a liver-colored cliff, commanding an empty lake and treeless barren land

probably unchanged for ten thousand years (except for the highway beneath it) is the face of a section of the basaltic lava covering the Columbia Plateau uplifted twenty-five hundred feet. Well to the east of it, a 50-mile-long block of the same lava beds has been raised to form Steens Mountain, a formation that, standing five thousand feet above the plain and usually snowcapped, seems as lonely as an errant iceberg.

On the opposite border of the Basin and Range Province, in southern New Mexico, is a fault-block mountain of a quite different kind still. The Guadalupe Range is a wedge of almost solid limestone, with its apex thrust like a lofty prow across the border into Texas to give that state its highest eminences. The eastern side of the wedge, containing the Carlsbad Caverns, is an uplifted section of the world's largest known fossil reef. Built up by coral, algae, and bryozoa millimeter by millimeter to heights of hundreds of feet, the reef for 350 miles bordered a lobe of the West Texas Basin, itself part of a retreating late Paleozoic sea—more recently a prolific source of petroleum. At the very point of the wedge, with a high mesa of layered sandstone for a pedestal, El Capitan stands more than eight thousand feet above sea level, its last one thousand feet rising sheer like a white citadel. Behind it, Guadalupe Peak stands at 8,750 feet. Overlooking the sand desert of the Pecos plains, the desiccated barrens of western Texas, and the bitter Salt Basin, the Guadalupes' pine-clad summits, falling off into stream-cut canyons, have been called an oasis in the clouds.

With all the heterogeneity of its antecedents, there is a certain homogeneity about the Basin and Range Province. The ranges typically take the form of long island mountains in sealike, if waterless, plains—plains for which they supplied the material. "An army of caterpillars marching north out of Mexico," Captain Dutton called them in one of the most quoted utterances of geology. The image is a curious one, for there is nothing lowly about these upturned giant blocks, emaciated as they may be: they rise to at least eleven thousand feet in five of the six states lying partly—or wholly, as in the case of Nevada—within the province. However, at the altitudes common to them they are able to extract twenty or thirty inches of yearly precipitation from the depleted clouds. Thus their backs are usually furred with conifers, which is what Dutton may have had in mind. So enormous has been the erosion that the basins occupy much more of the province than the ranges do.

The basins of the northern part belong to the sagebrush. A sage grouse, as a matter of fact, could walk from California almost across Wyoming without wanting for the leaves that make up its fodder. This part of the province, along with some adjacent areas, has been known as the Great Basin ever since Frémont named it that, having recognized it as an area of internal drainage from which no streams emerge (an area more than three times the size of New England, moreover). In the lower part of the Basin and Range Province, lying within the region called the Southwest, the basins make up what is popularly thought of as the desert, a

place not only perennially parched but of days that are furnace-hot in summer and mild in winter and of sparse and exotic vegetation.

The ponderous spasms that broke up the earth's crust in the central Cordilleran region must have been at their most intense toward the southwest, for it is there that the crust was raised to its maximum elevation and depressed to its minimum; the highest and lowest points in the forty-eight states are only eighty-three miles apart. Death Valley's depth—it is 280 feet below sea level at its lowest point—is matched in a long valley to the south of it. But the Salton Sink (a former name) is actually a sea floor fortuitously isolated. What happened was that at a time when the Gulf of California ran clear up to the San Bernardino Mountains west of Los Angeles, the silt-laden Colorado River, which emptied into it 150 miles below, built a delta all the way across it. In time the water behind the delta disappeared, leaving a deep trough. Then in 1905 the Colorado broke through an irrigation opening in a dike and before it could be stemmed—which took two years—created a lake in the trough. Called the Salton Sea, this is today, after slow shrinkage, thirty miles long and a third as wide. Another thing: the figure given for the depth of Death Valley refers merely to the level of the sediments forming its surface. The extent to which the block flooring the valley was dropped is indicated by the thickness of those sediments, which is probably about seven thousand feet.

"Good-bye, Death Valley," said a member of the first party of whites—forty-niners—to traverse the appalling sink, turning for a last look across the flats in which they had nearly died of starvation. The valley they had thus permanently branded is the archetype of the desert basin. No other place on earth combines such heat with such aridity. An astonishingly pleasant, green, winter resort has, it is true, been brought to pass on Furnace Creek, but to the south, from the mouth of Desolation Canyon, you can look down the valley and see not a living thing. What impresses you with lasting vividness is the fate of mountains without a vegetative cover. If those walling the valley had been merely ridges of varicolored clays unmercifully pelted by downpours, they would look much as they do. The hills rising at close hand behind you from bases like a succession of paws or knuckled fists are so deeply gullied that in places only thin walls separate the gullies. On the other side of the valley, from the mouths of the ravines that score the face of the high, fault-block range called the Panamints, alluvial fans slope down to the valley floor. Formed of detritus washed down from the heights, the fans are analogous to the deltas of rivers. But where rivers ordinarily flow continuously across their deposits, spreading them nearly flat, the evanescent torrents that feed the alluvial fans of desert ranges more often than not sink into them, even though a rimming of mesquite may show that they ooze out again at the foot. Thus the fans are comparatively steep, like sections of broad cones. Generally, too, as at the base of the Panamints, the fans run one into another, forming an undulating apron. This is such a conspicuous element of the topography of the region that "Range,

Apron, and Valley Province" would be a more descriptive term than the one employed.

While a basin valley may appear flat, it typically slopes down to the foot of the apron. It is from there that any water collecting in the basin last disappears. Many of the basins once held lakes. In fact, in the cooler, wetter times from twenty thousand years ago back a million or so more, considerable parts of the Basin and Range Province were under water. Great Salt Lake was ten times its present extent; its old shorelines can be detected one thousand feet up the Wasatch Mountains. Western Nevada might even have been described as a land of fiords, thanks to the huge lake that filled its lowlands; Walker and Pyramid lakes, among others, are its survivors. As shown by shorelines on its bordering mountains, Death Valley itself was filled to a depth of six hundred feet by a lake which may have reached the San Bernardino Mountains, 140 miles to the south. Even today, Great Salt remains the largest lake in the United States apart from the Great Lakes themselves. However, as a consequence of continuing evaporation, it has become four times as salty as the ocean and no animals but brine shrimp and some insect larvae can live in it. Most surviving basin lakes are at least brackish. But the great majority have dried up and any water that accumulates in them soon vanishes—lastly from the area at the foot of the apron called the *playa*, from the Spanish for "beach." Because in doing so it leaves behind its content of dissolved salts, the typical playa is an alkali flat—and cruel must have been the disillusionment of many a trailblazer of the West drawn to one of these sterile, shimmering expanses by thinking that any downhill course can lead only to water.

The road to the Sierra Nevada—the Snowy Serrates—that crosses Death Valley takes you through landscapes suitable to the various levels and degrees of purgatory. On either side, the fault-block ranges you go up and over via 5,000-foot passes look not only uninhabited but as if no mortals had ever approached their gnarled flanks. Even the flatlands in their shadows are lonely and desolate beyond comparison. The Amargosas and Panamints framing Death Valley look as if they had been gone over with a blowtorch. Volcanic rock is everywhere. Mountainsides in the Panamints have heavy scatterings of rounded, basaltic boulders as if they had been bombarded with them (in some cases they may have been, though basaltic sills and dikes are apt to break up and weather to rounded pieces). In the Inyo Range beyond, you ask yourself where such mountains of volcanic rocks could have come from. Many of the black boulders appear to have been greased, the coating being in fact of basaltic glass, from their rapid cooling when they were blasted from some crater's mouth.

It is over the Inyos that you have your first view of the Sierra Nevada. The sight transports you out of yourself. The band of white peaks stretches to the north and south at an incredible altitude. The slopes below the array being the same dusty blue as the sky, it seems to float above the earth. And the sense of unreality persists when you descend to Owens Valley to the remnant of the lake, now surrounded by salt flats as white as the Sierra's summits, that once covered it for 150 miles. From a drab, flat foreground, the ramparts rise directly to seven or eight thousand feet above the valley. Within ten miles, where eleven peaks rise over fourteen thousand feet, the difference approaches eleven thousand feet. The range seems to have no more relationship with the plain than a theatrical backdrop with the stage. (And it is a backdrop that looks as if it had been rendered by a master painter who had never seen a mountain.) A series of jaggedly pyramidal, granite forms with crests breaking through the snow and slopes etched with snow, braced by pediments like huge, conical hooves, conically toed, they go on by the hour as you drive north on U.S. 395. For many miles the Inyos continue on your right, scorched for lack of the precipitation the Sierra denies them. But there is a surprise. At their end, as if through one consuming effort, the earth has shouldered up the block of the White Mountains to rival the Sierra in height; their highest is only 250 feet lower than Mount Whitney, which stands at almost 14,500 feet. You cannot help exclaiming to yourself what a country this is that can spring on you a mountain range higher than Pikes Peak that you have never heard of.

Route 395 takes you up into the ponderosa pine forest and over passes eight thousand feet high, where the sun shines warm and air blows cold and clear. It takes you up along the foot of granite mountainsides of Gothic architecture, formed as of pulpits crowded together, and lets you see how cruelly riven the granite is in vertical fissures. It takes you, too, through a vol-

canic area: there is the Volcanic Glass Flow; there are the Mono Craters, which include some of the world's finest examples of rhyolitic pumice cones and lava domes; there is the Devils Postpile, in which is demonstrated the propensity of basalt for hardening in three- to seven-sided columns of astonishing regularity. However, it does not take you across the Sierra. There are roads that will, but this is a range on which four feet of snow may descend in a single fall, and except for a few months of the year you cannot count on getting across until you have gone more than two-thirds of the way from the southern end of the range to the northern, past its highest parts. There, the principal trans-Sierran highway passes close to the place where the Donner party was fatally trapped by early snows in October 1846.

A hundred miles farther north, at the end of the declining Sierra, there rises the generally white, 10,457-foot dome of the volcano Snow Butte, or Lassen Peak. The highest of several outgrowths from the slopes of an older and once taller volcano, Snow Butte is famous as a "plug-dome." Volcanoes of this type—of which Mont Pelée was one—are very dangerous. They are like champagne bottles when they go off, with the cork a mountain-sized plug of rock that shatters into bits and the froth an incandescent mass of gas, rock fragments, and lava dust. Snow Butte's last eruptions, between 1914 and 1921, were comparatively innocuous. They made it, however, the most recently active volcano in the country. It stands, in addition, as the outpost of the great volcanic province of the Northwest.

WHERE THE
ICE HAS BEEN

Reporting his discovery on the shores of Lake Superior of boulders representing sixty-four different kinds of rock, a geologist in 1793 found it almost impossible to believe that they "should be formed in one place" and concluded that "they must, therefore, have been conveyed there by some extraordinary means." Given the times, the writer's opinion as to the means was almost a foregone conclusion: "some mighty convulsion of nature."

The phenomenon was far wider and more manifold than the reference to the stones beside Lake Superior would suggest. Rocks and the detritus of rocks had unaccountably been spread over most of the northern landscapes. As James D. Dana was to describe it, "The drift was one of the most stupendous events in geological history. In some way, by a cause as wide as the continent—and, I may say, as wide nearly as the world—stones of all sizes, to immense boulders of one to two thousand tons weight, were transported along with gravel and sand, over hills and valleys, deeply scratching the rocks across which they travelled." Dana did not exaggerate. The Madison Boulder, in New England, a block of granite weighing over nine million pounds, was transported two miles from its place of origin. Most of the "erratics" are from nearby sources, but many are found to have come at least three hundred miles; the record is eight hundred.

Through the first half of the nineteenth century and beyond geologists puzzled over the "drift." They were not, of course, altogether without recourse: there had, it was said, been "a general current which, at some unknown

period, flowed impetuously across the whole continent of North America." "There cannot remain a doubt but that a violent current of water has rushed over the surface. . . ." But currents that could lift great boulders over hills while also dragging them over rock ledges so that the surfaces of both were polished and grooved were difficult to visualize. It was a Connecticut businessman, Peter Dobson, who in 1825 first grasped the essential principle. After watching excavations for a new cotton mill, he wrote a letter to Benjamin Silliman, soon published in the *American Journal of Science*, in which he suggested that the erratics could have been worn flat on one side and also furrowed only if they had been dragged over both rocks and earth underwater while held in one position in ice. Perhaps because the letter-writer lacked credentials, little attention was paid to his theory until, seventeen years later, Roderick Murchison addressed the Geologic Society of London, commending "the terse argument of Peter Dobson, a previous acquaintance with which might have saved volumes of disputation."

Dobson had been able to think only of icebergs as the agency by which the rocks had been moved, and these were clearly inadequate. It remained for a brilliant young Swiss zoologist, Louis Agassiz, to conceive of the form the ice would have had to take and to perceive fully the implications. It came to him in 1836 on a hiking trip in the Rhone Valley with his friend Jean de Charpentier. The purpose of the trip was to follow up Charpentier's notion that the Alpine glaciers had once been of much

greater extent and had deposited the heaps of sand, gravels, and clay and the erratics that bestrewed the lower valleys of the Alps and even the Piedmont—for it was a peculiarity of the "drift" that it occurred not only in the northern latitudes but in and around lofty mountain ranges farther south. Skeptical to begin with, Agassiz was seized by a vision that went far beyond any his friend had entertained. Before his gaze there unfolded the spectacle of a glacier beside which the shrunken ice fields of Greenland and the Arctic regions, "formidable as they seem to us," as he was to say later, are "but as the patches of snow and ice lingering on the north side of our hills after the spring has opened." Over northern Europe and Asia, "previously covered with a rich vegetation and peopled with large mammalia," he declared in an address the year following the Rhone excursion, "Siberian winter established itself. . . . Death enveloped all nature in a shroud."

By 1842, Charles Lyell and Charles Darwin had been convinced, but while the glacial theory stood alone in accounting for all the observable facts of the "drift," no one conversant with human nature need be surprised that resistance to it was strong. (Probably it should occasion little surprise either that Agassiz, innovator though he was and luminary of American science as a teacher at Harvard for twenty-seven years, refused to the end to accept the import of Darwin's *Origin of Species*.) Nevertheless, though no one could explain satisfactorily how the conditions required to produce the ice sheet could have arisen, the witnesses of

It was the gifted, Swiss-born naturalist Louis Agassiz who first conceived the idea of a great age of glaciers and recognized the effect they had had on the landscape. The illustrations at right show mountains before, during, and after glaciation, and how the advancing ice carved a V-shaped valley into a U-shape, while leaving a "hanging valley" (note waterfall, bottom drawing). Hollows left on upper mountain slopes are known as cirques.

its visitation proved simply impossible to gainsay and by the 1880's the holdouts had very largely come around. It is now taken as fact that in the Pleistocene period, during the past million years or so (estimates run over two million), ice sheets blanketed northern Europe (Scandinavia, Great Britain south to London, northern Germany, Poland, and northern Russia) and in North America extended south to northern New Jersey, northern Pennsylvania, roughly to the Ohio and Missouri rivers and in the Far West for a short distance over the Canadian border. The Alps and Pyrenees and the higher ranges in Asia and the United States were also glaciated, and this devastation was unleashed upon our hemisphere not just once but four times in the Pleistocene period. Oceanic sediments indicate that similar ice movements took place in the Southern Hemisphere. Moreover, unmistakable signs of earlier ice ages have come to light. These are in the form of "tillites"—rocks formed of the heterogeneous scrapings of the glacier known as till. Buried for long periods and sometimes resting on grooved ledges, these indicate that there was a Precambrian ice age and also a Permian, in the late Paleozoic era. The tillites of the latter are the more provocative. These have been unearthed in southern Australia, South Africa, southern Madagascar, southern India, the eastern ranges of the Andes in Argentina, Uruguay, southern Brazil, and tropical Bolivia. Unless there was an ice sheet of fantastically improbable distribution, those scattered regions must have been adjacent well down in the Southern Hemisphere 200 million

Much of the continent's most awesome scenery is the result of glacial erosion. At left is Yosemite Valley, California, a classic example. The glacial origins of the U-shaped valley were first recognized by conservationist John Muir (right), who, starting in 1868, spent six years exploring and studying Yosemite, which he called the "most holy mansion of mountains." Muir later discovered and described many of the great Alaskan glaciers.

years ago—while Greenland luxuriated in subtropical vegetation. And if they were, then the theory of continental dispersion is established.

Why the earth should at times have become partially glaciated remains a subject of much speculation. The grim phenomenon has been ascribed variously to the shifting configuration of landmasses, a change in the position of the poles, the varying amounts of carbon dioxide and volcanic dust in the atmosphere, variations in the earth's position relative to the sun, the passage of the solar system through clouds of cosmic dust, and fluctuations in the amount of the sun's radiation. However, these hypotheses are all either open to critical objection or such as have proved impossible to verify. And what complicates the problem is that not only must prevailing temperatures fall to produce an ice age—or so most geologists are agreed—but evidently precipitation must increase.

Yet it has happened repeatedly that for periods of thousands of years at a time conditions have been such that substantially more snow has fallen in the high latitudes and altitudes during the winters than has melted during the summers. And that is all that is required. Snow granulates with age, and as it accumulates and is compacted by its own weight the granules are recrystallized into ice, much as sedimentary rock becomes recrystallized at extreme depths into denser, harder rock. Ice formed in this manner tends to be bluish because of the air it contains. Under sufficient pressure it becomes plastic. In this, again, there is an analogy with rock, which is not surprising, since ice is no less a mineral than quartz or feldspar.

With ice, however, plasticity sets in at comparatively modest pressures, under ice no more than fifty feet deep. And becoming plastic, ice starts to flow—downhill or out from under.

On top of the illimitable reaches of time and incalculable forces geology requires the mind to encompass, there are the snows of the Pleistocene. The snows were not continuous, certainly, and even in the ice ages' vast realms of perpetual winter there must have been warmth in the normally summer months and considerable thawing; but even then a white and lifeless scene would have stretched from horizon to horizon for thousands of miles. For the snows, if not unremitting, were all but inexhaustible. The snow fell patiently and quietly or poured in on blizzard winds, and to provide the water for the little white flakes the oceans shrank in their beds. And still it snowed. And when it stopped, it stopped only to resume. For periods exceeding the span of human history the long and bitter winters brought snowstorm upon snowstorm. By the time the maximum amount of water held in the snow-formed ice had been reached, the depleted oceans had dropped several hundred feet all around the world. Treeless plains hundreds of miles from north to south connected Siberia and Alaska, enabling North America to exchange the horse for man; Alaska, except in the extreme south, and Siberia were largely unglaciated owing to the aridity of their climates.

The ice reached its greatest depth not where the cold was most intense but where cold combined favorably with precipitation. One such dome covered Scandinavia. In North America

there seems to have been one over Labrador and another west of Hudson Bay. From these centers, the ice spread out like batter, but batter of rocklike consistency and augmented as it went by further blanketings of snow. No one knows at what speed the dreadful ice front moved. Probably its advance was exceedingly slow, though where the ice funneled through a gap in a mountain barrier against which the main mass had piled up, it may have approached the speed of some glaciers in Alaska and Greenland today, which have been known to advance 150 feet a day. But whatever its rate, it was irresistible. Whatever mountain ranges it did not overtop it breached—and apart from the highest of the Northern Rockies it overtopped them all as far as it went. Like a continent-wide bulldozer, it scraped the land to bedrock, and where the bedrock was soft, scooped it out as well.

Pushing through new terrain, or reconquering terrain from which it had withdrawn perhaps centuries or more before, its front may have been largely or wholly concealed by a debris of forests, earth, and boulders. Even when the rate of melting at the margins equaled the rate of the ice's advance, rock, gravel, and other spoil would have been carried forward to the static front as by a conveyor belt. The glacier's most effective scouring tools were the rocks it picked up and held fast against its underside or the flanks of its lobes. These it would have wrenched from outcrops. In general the glacier smoothed, polished, and grooved the forward slopes and sides of the hills and mountains it overran and stripped away their rearward slopes, leaving them steep and blocky. Until themselves worn smooth, rocks thus quarried—house-sized or minute—would have served as the teeth of a rasp.

In the early stages of a glacial age, as the ice sheet was built up, so were glaciers in the mountains to the south of it. Those the ice sheet later reached were incorporated in it, but there were huge ones hundreds of miles beyond its farthest advance. The precipitation that created vast lakes in the Basin and Range Province and turned the desert verdant fell as snow on the higher ranges, all but burying them in ice.

Some conception of the alpine glaciers of the Pleistocene can be gained from living models today. There are small glaciers even in the Southern Rockies and Sierra Nevada. To the north, glaciers reach three hundred feet in thickness in Glacier National Park and are spawned plentifully in the higher Cascades; one of the many on Mount Rainier is a mile wide and four long. The closer to the Arctic, the lower the glaciers come down in the valleys. At the head of the fiords of the Alaskan panhandle, where they attain thicknesses of thousands of feet, glaciers meet the sea; Muir Glacier does so in a vertical face over 250 feet above the water, into which it has been estimated to discharge thirty million cubic feet of ice a day in summer. (Glacier Bay, as it is called, is incorporated in the second largest unit in the National Park system.) To the northeast, fed by glaciers up to fifty miles long, Malaspina Glacier spreads an ice field fifteen hundred square miles below Mount St. Elias.

The formation of the Great Lakes in the late Pleistocene involved thousands of years of scouring by a series of glaciers, with the modern shore-lines emerging only about twenty-five hundred years ago. The maps show how transitional lakes collected in former river beds as the glaciers retreated northward, and, as indicated by arrows, how patterns of drainage changed with time. The last map shows the lakes after the glaciers retreated.

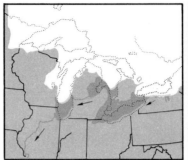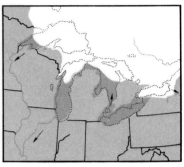

What is immediately apparent about alpine glaciers is that they prey on the mountains that harbor them. Like great white leeches they gnaw away at their hosts. The strippage begins high up at the very head of the valley in which the glacier arises. As the snow that feeds it is compacted, the ice that is formed freezes to the rock wall and when it sags downhill pulls rocks away with it. Meltwater flowing by day into the gap thus opened seeps through rocks and, subsequently freezing, loosens more blocks. These topple to the glacier's bed or are pulled away when new snow fills the gap and the glacier slips again. Armed with rocks embedded in its bottom and sides, the glacier gouges its way along in the manner of the continental ice sheet. It sharpens contours at its source, where it collects rocks, and smoothes them out below, where it uses them for grinding. The effects are likely to be concealed in the case of existing glaciers, though conspicuous enough where their giant Pleistocene predecessors had their way, but the masses of rubble at a glacier's snout leave no doubt of the toll of rocks it is taking. That which is carried along its sides is sufficient to preserve its identity when several flow together, as is common in well-glaciated terrain; compound glaciers are streaked with till so that from a distance they resemble broad, multilane concrete highways. Where a glacier has shrunk (and most of them have shrunk greatly in the past century and a half or two) there will be ridges of till—unsorted clay, sand, gravel, and rocks—in front of it, each marking a former terminus.

A plateau of ice today covers almost seven hundred thousand square miles of Greenland and another some five million of Antarctica to a depth of up to ten thousand feet. Those who have beheld these remnants of the Pleistocene ice sheet have some idea of what it must have been like to stand at its foot. Stone age men on both sides of the Atlantic were well acquainted with it and with the inclement climates it brought; under its frigid breath tundra spread where oaks and maples now grow, and dark northern forests stretched far to the south of it. A blood-chilling apparition it must have been, towering above the mountains of debris heaped before it, glittering in the sun in the thin arctic air or disappearing overhead in the snow-laden clouds. From the shore, then many miles east of where it is today, the blue-white wall of ice would have been seen stretching off across the Atlantic. Now and again sections of its face would have fallen away to shatter on the floe-laden water below, and huge masses, breaking off from below, would have come wallowing to the surface to right themselves and drift away.

At times of prolonged warmth, rivers of meltwater, cutting deep beds in the ice, would have poured in cataracts from the failing, stricken monster, washing the till across the stony, muddy plains left bare by the ice's contraction. From within it would have come the roar of waters plunging a thousand feet sheer through interior cavities. Lichens and mosses, followed by grasses and herbs, then prostrate shrubs and willows, would have commenced the revegetation of the barren lands. With them, herds of grazers and browsers would have appeared—chunky, woolly mammoths

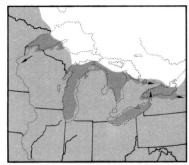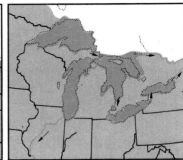

with thatch-domed heads and immense, near-circular tusks; the rangier mastodons; musk-oxen; giant bison and giant moose; and, prey-ing on the herbivores, huge dire wolves and sa-ber-toothed cats the size of lions. Behind them were giant beavers and giant ground sloths. (Thomas Jefferson had some ground sloth bones with him, found in western Virginia, when he read a memoir on them before the American Philosophical Society in Philadelphia.)

But in winter the sound of rushing, thunder-ing waters resounding from the ice sheet would have been stilled. And the time would have come when prevailing temperatures in the north would have dropped a few degrees. Then, obedient to the pressures of the incom-prehensible volumes of deepening ice behind it, and with sharp, recurrent cries of wrenched or riven rock and the reverberant crack of ice splitting in crevasses, the Thing would have begun to move again, carrying all before it.

The ice stood two miles deep over New Eng-land. And it was enduring, bearing down upon the continent with all its brutal weight for tens of millennia. Moreover, to the ravages it wrought, which nothing in its path escaped, the country was subjected not just once but four times; of that one has to keep reminding oneself. Four times the crushing plateau of ice pushed down from the north, on each return after scores or hundreds of thousands of years of mild temperatures, when deep topsoil would long since have re-formed on the skinned earth and the wasted lands would have been re-claimed by crowded forests all the way to the Arctic. The four ice sheets seem to have ad-vanced nearly to the same lines, except that the fourth did not go quite as far as its prede-cessors in most of the eastern half of the coun-try, particularly in the Middle West. (For some reason, southwestern Wisconsin was bypassed by all the ice sheets.) The fourth got under way between forty and fifty thousand years ago and began receding probably about fifteen thousand years ago. If, as is possible, it is still receding, the ice age itself cannot yet have come to an end.

As far as it reached, the ice sheet radically altered the continent's pattern of waterways. A lobe of the sheet filled the canyon of the Co-lumbia in north-central Washington, turning the river southward. In the basaltic strata of the Columbia Plateau the river cut a new can-yon, known today as the Grand Coulee, be-tween one mile and fifteen miles wide and up to a thousand feet deep. Before the recession of the ice sheet had reopened its previous bed, the Columbia, swollen with meltwater, poured through the Grand Coulee over a waterfall nearly three miles wide and four hundred feet deep with, as has been said, the roar of a thousand Niagaras. To the east, the rivers that once had carried the runoff of the eastern slopes of the mountains of Montana and the Central Rockies to Hudson Bay were blocked. Skirting the edge of the ice sheet, they formed a new river: the upper Missouri. The Ohio was shifted well to the south of its erstwhile course; like the Missouri, it flowed along the base of the sheet to the Mississippi.

During the millennia-long initial stages of the Great Thaw the Father of Waters must have carried enormous torrents seaward. Its tributaries drained the ice sheet along a 2,000-mile front. Then, as this front retreated, it received the drainage of the nascent Great Lakes, notably the meltwater of the lobes of the glacier that had formed their beds. In place of the Great Lakes there had been, in pre-Pleistocene times, simply large river valleys. These valleys, into which the glacier presumably first flowed, were the last parts from which it disappeared. The lakes came gradually into being as the lobes shrank back. According to carbon 14 dating, this took place only about eleven thousand years ago. The initial outlets were at the tip of Lake Michigan, into the Chicago River, and at the tip of Lake Superior, into the St. Croix. With the uncovering of Lake Erie, volumes of water began to pour eastward into the Mohawk and then seaward via the Hudson. It was a very long time before the St. Lawrence outlet opened up to take the entire discharge of the system. And meanwhile the Mississippi was taking the overflow of a lake that had formed to the northwest in front of the receding ice sheet, which was blocking the area's natural drainage to Hudson Bay. Lake Manitoba and Lake Winnipeg are among the largest of the continent, after the Great Lakes, but they and the Red Lakes of northern Minnesota are mere remnants of that freshwater inland sea, named Lake Agassiz by geologists, which may have covered one hundred thousand square miles, or more than the combined area of the five present Great Lakes.

There was nothing precipitate about the ice sheet's withdrawal, at least not in the earlier stages. Analysis of cores from lake bottoms (in which summer and winter deposits are different, making it possible to count yearly layers back from the present) shows that the retreat of the front from the vicinity of Hartford, Connecticut, to St. Johnsbury, Vermont, a scant 190 miles, took forty-three hundred years.

"Scenically," says William C. Putnam, "the world is more indebted to glaciation than to any other process of erosion." Alpine scenery the world over is the product of the Pleistocene ice ages. In the mountains, the glaciers hollowed out the slopes whence they arose, leaving spectacular concave sweeps of rock wall generally known as *cirques*. These are especially prominent in Glacier National Park, but even the Appalachians provide a well-known example in Tuckerman Ravine on the side of Mount Washington. Chiseled away on their sides, mountains became sunken of slope and sharper of ridge—more peaked. The Matterhorn is the classic case, and its name has been taken to designate all of its type, such as Mount Assiniboine, an 11,870-foot, particularly noble and forbidding matterhorn in the Canadian Rockies near Banff.

Mountain topography was accentuated everywhere that glaciers invaded it, so long as the mountains rose above them. (It was because they were overtopped by the ice sheet that New England's highest ranges are rounded of summit despite the carving away of some of their flanks by alpine glaciers.) It is possibly illuminative of a central truth about life that the adversity to which mountains are exposed and that ultimately is fatal to them is what gives them form, beauty, and meaning. Without the ceaseless attack of water in its various forms, the earth's upheaved masses of rock would remain shapeless, incoherent, chaotic jumbles. If nothing else prompted such a reflection, the Grand Tetons would. They may be, of all the mountains in the country, the most thrilling. Dramatic enough to begin with as a fault-block uptilted at least seven thousand feet above its surroundings on the east, the range has been gouged so deep by glaciers and running water that in many places the eastward-flowing streams originate from three to five miles west of the major summits. Brought into extreme relief, the peaks resemble, at a distance that brings the whole group into view, flames of rock and snow licking skyward.

Those cirques at the heads of the valleys and deep, broad troughs plowed out of their lower reaches; in such did the alpine glaciers of the Pleistocene display their might. The characteristic U-shaped valleys may be found from New England—Franconia Notch being a notable example—to California, where the Tuolumne, Merced, and Kings rivers flow through canyons scooped deep out of the Sierra Nevada batholith. The display of granite in the walls of such canyons is almost overpowering. In Yosemite Valley, Rock Chief (or El Capitan) and North Dome rise almost sheer for thirty-five hundred feet above the Merced. There, too, are spectacularly exhibited "hanging valleys" such as remain when a glacier has excavated a trunk valley to a new depth and the branch valleys and the streams that cut them are left to empty into thin air high up its sides. Six of the

Merced's tributaries drop more than three hundred feet from hanging valleys, Ribbon Falls being over sixteen hundred feet in height and Yosemite Creek cascading almost twenty-five hundred feet in two stages. It was probably in part the glistening, glacially polished mountainsides that John Muir had in mind when he called the Sierra "the Range of Light."

"Land of Infinite Variety" says a sign welcoming you to South Dakota. The claim is one that the visitor may well consider to be on the brave side. The grasslands of the western part of the state, undulating with the swell of the Great Plains, are as interminable as the wind that blows across them. Lark buntings and western meadowlarks sing bravely in a landscape devoid of the cover a single shrub would afford, except where a cluster of farm buildings and trees stands like an islet in the ocean. But across the Missouri, north of the city of Pierre, small boulders in the fields mark the start of the drift and presage a change. Ahead, to the east as to the north, are ponds and small lakes, indigo under the clear northern sky and tenanted by ducks, grebes, and wading birds. Minnesota and Wisconsin are lands of lakes, as is most of Canada east of the Great Plains; large parts of Manitoba, Ontario, and Quebec are almost as much water as land. By digging out valleys in plains and mountains and plugging existing valleys with its deposits, the ice sheet was an indefatigable creator of lakes and, where the sea invaded the troughs it had left, of fiords, as on the coasts of Norway, British Columbia, and the Alaskan panhandle.

As it excavated, so did the glacier pile up.

123

Cape Cod, Martha's Vineyard,
Nantucket, and Long Island are
the products of glaciers
that began building in Labrador
in the late Pleistocene and,
in time, sent immense scallop-
shaped ice fronts across New
England gathering countless
tons of rock and soil. When
the long glacial age ended
and the ice had withdrawn,
the rubble was left behind
creating new land formations.
Map shows the glaciers' direction
of flow and southern limit.

Kames is the name (Scottish) given to the conical hills of gravel dumped at the foot of its wa-
terfalls; *eskers* (Irish) is given to the ridges of
gravel, sometimes many miles in length and resembling sinuous railroad embankments, that
were once the beds of rivers coursing through
it. And then there are *drumlins* (of uncertain
etymology). The battles of Breed's and Bunker
hills were fought from drumlins. There are
swarms of them in upstate New York and in
southeastern Wisconsin, along with other
striking relics of the last ice sheet, including
sections of the terminal moraines. Drumlins
are roughly semi-spindle-shaped, at most half a
mile long and 150 feet high, of glacial till with a
heavy proportion of sticky clay. Lined up as
they are in the direction of the glacier's advance, they were evidently formed beneath it.
But how they were formed still remains unclear today.

The major accumulations from the ice sheet
were the moraines along its margins. Where it
stood still for a long time at the stage of its farthest invasion, its forward motion balanced by
its rate of melting, the ridge of till built up
there was likely to be enormous. Usually such
stability was lacking and the till was dispersed,
leaving a hummocky kind of terrain, often
with ponds or lakes in the hollows of a kind
called kettleholes; these remained where a half-
buried mass of ice, left behind in the glacier's
contraction, took many years to melt. But by
far the larger part of the mud, sand, and gravel
that went into the moraines was spread far and
wide by erosion, the first and doubtless most
drastic agency having been the water that flood-

ed down through the centuries from the melting ice sheet itself. Spread across the land in
outwash plains, so termed, the finer material
was carried farthest, to form the flat, fertile
farmlands of the Middle West today. In addition, vast quantities of silt from the outwash
were picked up by the winds that howled
across the expanse of desolation overlooked by
the dirty, rotting masses of the receding ice
sheet and of the bergs that stood where it had
been, and this silt was spread over the grasslands beyond. Forming a loam called *loess*
(from an old Germanic word meaning to free or
to loosen) these silt deposits blanketed the
whole Mississippi Valley, here and there even
to depths of twenty or thirty feet.

The great morainal monuments are the maritime outriders of the Northeast. Rising from
the sea where no land would, had the ice sheet
not built it, they are the supreme witnesses of
its prodigious power. The terminal moraine
forms the backbone of Long Island, standing
as high as 410 feet above sea level south of
Huntington. (One hardly dares guess how high
the pile must originally have stood.) To the
east it breaks off at Montauk Point; to the
west, after a gap cut by the Hudson River and
spanned by the Verrazano-Narrows Bridge, it
forms part of Staten Island. A second recessional moraine, almost as high, deposited when
the ice sheet had withdrawn a space and then
returned nearly to its previous position, leads
off from the first one near Flushing and forms
the northern shore of Long Island, along the
Sound. Cut off at Orient Point, it reappears as
Plum Island and then as Fishers Island before

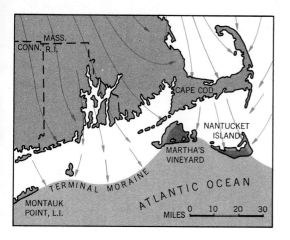

proceeding on along the coast of Rhode Island.

The terminal and recessional moraines that created Martha's Vineyard, Nantucket Island, and Cape Cod operated in a rather more complicated way. Here it was a matter not just of two stages of the ice sheet but of three lobes of it as well.

The westernmost of the three lobes, coming down through Massachusetts, spread out. While on one side it excavated the softer rock as it approached the coast to create Narragansett Bay, on the other, veering east, it dumped at its terminus a moraine that now forms the northwestern shore of Martha's Vineyard. As it receded, it dumped another to form the eastern shore of Buzzards Bay and the Elizabeth Islands group.

The terminal moraine of the central lobe of the three constitutes the northeastern shore of Martha's Vineyard and the northern shore of Nantucket, its recessional moraine the northern shore—the biceps—of Cape Cod's inner arm. The outer, eastern lobe, coming south well off the present shore (but down what was then the coastal plain), turned westward as it neared its finish line. There the moraine it left forms the eastern shore of Nantucket.

The upper arm of Cape Cod was formed between the central and outer lobes in their recessional phases when their facing edges stood some miles apart, separated by a gravelly, stony wasteland. Torrents of meltwater flowing from the two ice masses swept with them the till the ice had trucked down from the north and piled it up in an outwash plain between them. Layer upon layer, the plain was built up into a plateau which was joined at right angles to the moraine of the present cape's inner arm. Such is the picture given by a contemporary specialist in the subject, Barbara Blau Chamberlain.

Today there is no difficulty identifying the haphazard, sordid-looking conglomerations of clay and sand, studded with rocks, that make up the moraines. They are exposed in Sankaty Head in Nantucket, behind the beach at Cape Cod's Nauset Harbor, in the humpy cliffs of Montauk Point, and the headlands above Long Island Sound, whence rocks the size of small cabins have tumbled to the shore. You can recognize the well-washed till in the stern-visaged escarpment that rises from the outer beach along the forearm of Cape Cod like the front of a mesa, up to 170 feet high. And there are the outwash plains to the south of the moraines, some the sites of towns (including Brooklyn), some farmed, some grown up in forests of black oak and pitch pine, Nantucket's partly in moorland and bear-oak barrens. There are the kettleponds; the hind arm of Cape Cod is riddled with them. Wandering about in the maritime lands with geology on your mind you might almost expect to find a decaying hunk of the glacier—as one was unearthed the other day in Norway—so recent, comparatively, do the events of the last ice age seem. Yet what these vast earthworks of the ice sheet looked like to begin with we can have little idea, for through a century of centuries they have stood within the realm of that which equals the ice sheet in its power to despoil the land and transport the residues—the sea.

THE HUNGRY SEA

One hundred million years ago, in mid-Cretaceous times, the ocean came up to the foot of the Piedmont, halfway across the southeastern states. Farther south the coastline swung around the lower end of the Appalachians and ran due north to the southern tip of Illinois, then generally southwestward. Only in the Northeast did it lie farther out, probably, than it does now. The present coastal plains of the Atlantic and Gulf states were built up by sediments subsequently laid down on the floor of the shallow seas bordering the land. The old Mesozoic coastline in the East is marked today by the fall line, where the rivers tumble from the hard, plutonic rocks of the Piedmont to the channels they have cut all the way down to sea level in the softer sedimentary rocks of the coastal plain—thus permitting navigation all the way up to the falls from the ocean.

By the end of the Miocene period, twelve million years ago, the coastal plain, to a large extent, was raised above sea level. It continued, however, to be extended by sediments carried down by the rivers. The Mississippi alluvial plains from Illinois southward and the outer half of the coastal plain to the west, in Louisiana and Texas, were formed of such sediments only since the onset of the Pleistocene period. In this period, when perhaps fourteen million cubic miles of water may have been withdrawn from the oceans at one time and converted into ice, the sea retreated from its earlier shores. Mammoths taller than the largest African bull elephant trumpeted in sunny woodlands where today the only signs of ter-

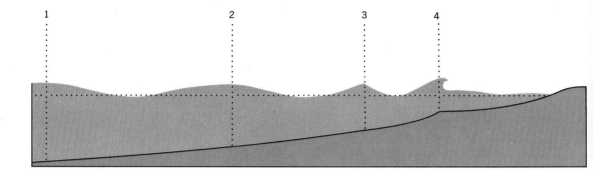

restrial life are the wreckages of sunken ships.

Four times the sea must have receded from much of the continental shelves and four times returned as the ice sheet melted, each time overwhelming under-drifting sands and sea-water marshes and forests, the haunts of a teeming land fauna. But the cumulative effect was more than the restoration of the sea to its own lost realm. The continental platform had been depressed under the stupendous burden of the ice it had borne for tens of thousands of years at a time. With the removal of the weight, it came back, but it has not come fully back—at least so far. (In Scandinavia, anyhow, it is known to be still rising.) The Great Thaw that began some fifteen thousand years in the past had by six thousand years ago sent the oceans over continental margins that had stood high and dry before the ice pushed them down. The coastal plain remains submerged from the Bay of New York northward. What had been green hills for millions of years are now banks over which trawlers ply a hundred miles and more offshore, among them Georges Banks off Cape Cod and the Grand Banks of Newfoundland.

North of the Bay of New York the coast is a "drowned" one. It is conspicuously such in Maine, where, on a map, the coastline looks frayed and fragmented. The land runs out to sea in peninsulas and islands that once were hilltops and the sea penetrates inland in far-reaching estuaries that once were valleys down which rivers flowed. While Maine has a seaboard only 240 miles long, it has a shoreline 3,000 miles long.

To the south are other great estuaries that came into being because, while the ocean level was several hundred feet lower than today, the rivers cut deeper and broader valleys in their lower reaches which the sea flooded when it returned. The Hudson, which is tidal to Albany, almost 150 miles inland, has a double bed, a broad upper one and a keel-like lower one, well below sea level, which the torrents flowing down it from the melting glaciers of the Great Lakes must have helped cut. Delaware Bay is an invaded river valley. Chesapeake Bay is a much larger one; the many rivers that empty into it, including the Susquehanna, Potomac, Rappahannock, York, and James, which also severally occupy drowned river valleys in their lower reaches, were once tributaries of a single river. Mobile Bay and Tampa Bay are other invaded river valleys, and so, in the West, is the double bay spanned at its narrow mouth by San Francisco's Golden Gate Bridge. The Pacific Coast from Washington northward has the character of a drowned coast, like that of Maine and also like that of Norway, where valleys plowed through mountains by glaciers were subsequently flooded to become fiords.

It is on a steep and rocky coast like that of Maine and of the Pacific Northwest that one is most aware of the sea's assault upon the continent. Waves break with full violence on the headlands of such a coast, where, by contrast, in running in above a shelving bottom they break offshore. And they break with stunning power. Waves themselves are relatively innocuous, there being little forward displacement of water in them. (Ripples running down a flag,

*The course of an ocean wave
is traced in the diagram
at left. At sea the height
of a wave (1) is one-twentieth
its length, crest to crest.
As it approaches the shore (2)
the drag of the ocean floor
reduces the wave's length to
twice the depth of the water.
The wave is then forced into
a peak (3), which breaks (4)
when its height and the depth
of the water are in a ratio
of approximately 3 to 4.
Overleaf: a dramatic climax.*

which are analogous, do so without affecting the texture of the medium at all.) Meeting a seawall, a wave will simply run up the obstruction and be reflected from it. A ship will ordinarily hoist up and pass beneath. But breakers are something else.

Waves become breakers when they reach a certain degree of steepness. Those rolling in on a coast slow down as they "feel the bottom" and, with others behind pressing upon them, "peak up." When a wave reaches a depth no more than about 1.3 times its height, it cannot lift enough water to fill itself out. Its front flattens, becomes concave, and its top, unsupported, plunges. A mass of heavy and incompressible water hurtles forward like a battering ram; a wave six feet high when it breaks can deliver a punch of three thousand pounds per square foot.

Such figures make more credible the reports of prodigious feats breakers have performed. One, striking at the entrance to the canal to Amsterdam harbor, picked up a concrete block of forty thousand pounds' weight and lifted it vertically, setting it on top of a pier almost five feet above high-water mark. Breakers have thrown rocks weighing nearly seven thousand pounds over a twenty-foot wall at Cherbourg. At Wick Breakwater, Scotland, a mass of stones set in concrete and bound by iron rods that weighed two and three-quarter million pounds was torn loose and moved bodily. The sheets of water cast up by breakers on their rebound testify as dramatically to their might. They have been known to envelop completely the 97-foot lighthouse on Minots Ledge, south

of Boston harbor—the earlier shaft, with its two keepers, having been carried away by breakers. The keeper of the light at Trinidad Head, California, in 1913, reported that a breaker striking the 195-foot cliff on which the light is situated sent a solid sea to a level with his eyes where he stood by the lantern. And at Tillimook Rock, Oregon, in 1902, a solid mass of water fell on the roof of the lighthouse dwelling, two hundred feet above sea level.

In the Northern Hemisphere the winds that raise the seas are prevailingly westerlies, and the Pacific Coast of the United States from northern California northward, like the corresponding coast of Europe, is exposed to waves with a "fetch" the width of an ocean. Henry B. Bigelow and W. T. Edmondson, in a publication issued by the U.S. Navy Hydrographic Office, estimate that the seas battering the coast with breakers forty feet and probably even sixty feet high are as heavy as any in the world. The easterly storms that send the seas against our northeastern coasts, they point out, rarely persist long enough to build up surf more than twelve to fifteen feet high. Still, these eastern waves are capable of cutting clear through a barrier island, tearing down homes and demolishing sand dunes, as did the Ash Wednesday storm of 1962. Moreover, our Atlantic and Gulf coasts are subject to hurricanes and their accompanying waves, which are particularly devastating to low-lying coasts. On September 8, 1900, storm waves probably twenty-five feet high on top of a tide fifteen feet above normal plunged in upon Galveston, Texas, and killed upwards of five thousand

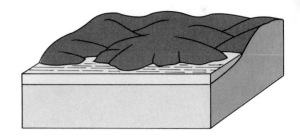

persons. About six hundred died on the southern coast of New England in the furiously destructive equinoctial hurricane of 1938. In 1967, Hurricane Beulah flooded a quarter of the state of Texas and did damage in the hundreds of millions of dollars.

Such is the weaponry leveled at the frontiers of the continent; no less effective, however, in some stretches is the day-to-day, minute-by-minute working-over the sea gives the shores. Water in motion is the agency of change, and water along the shore is in perpetual motion. The all-embracing circulatory system of the oceans, of which the Gulf Stream is a prominent part, helps keep it so. So do the tides; tidal currents round the tip of Cape Cod at 1.8 knots and pour through the Golden Gate at between 3.0 and 4.0. But the most telling propellants of the water are the waves, of which eight thousand a day break upon the shore.

The object of the sea, pursued with a consistency of purpose no less determined for being mindless, is to produce a regular coastline with a beach of low profile composed of fine materials, and this is but a way-stage, one must suppose, in the ultimate elimination of all land. Our southeastern coast, with its long, low, straight beaches and gentle, offshore gradient represents a condition to which all coasts would come if the continents were inert. On such coasts a considerable degree of equilibrium has been reached between marine and continental forces—not a static equilibrium, but a condition of low tension and of give-and-take on both sides. Where the shore rises in bulwarks of rock, the confrontation is at an initial stage and is severe, and the tension is high.

The latter kind of shore—an immature shore—calls into play the sea's full arsenal. Slamming into the cliff, the breakers trap air in its fissures, and this air, compressed, delivers the full blow of the breaker against the sides of the fissures. Where a shore has been tunneled into, as at the Thunderhole in Mount Desert Island, off the coast of Maine, the smashing of full-sized waves into the recess shakes the earth. Under repeated blows, the rocks are dislodged and the shore-cliff undermined. The zone of surf is a source of missiles for storm breakers to hurl against the still-standing rocks and a ball mill of boulders, cobbles, and smaller stones in perpetual process of collision. Through such punishment the stoutest rocks are destined to be chipped and worn down and end as grains of sand. These grains themselves, unless lifted beyond the waves' reach and subjected to mutual abrasion under the wind's lash, are said to be virtually immortal, being shielded from contact with one another by the film of water that envelops each, even on a seemingly hard-packed beach.

When rocks of different types compose the coast, the yielding of the softer will leave the harder in promontories. These are, however, doomed. Against them the sea's energies are concentrated. Sometimes the promontory is severed at its base, forming a "stack," perhaps with an arch connecting it with the mainland as an intermediate stage. Such sections of the cut-back cliff are a characteristic feature of the coast of our Pacific Northwest.

The focusing of the seas upon protrusions of

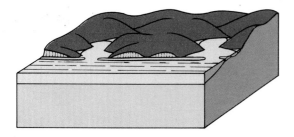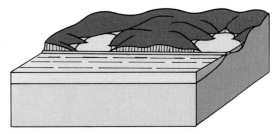

the coast comes about through refraction, as it is called, which affects waves of all kinds, including light waves. In encountering a more resistant medium at an angle, the course of the waves is altered to bring it more nearly into perpendicular with the edge of the new medium, which means that the waves themselves will become more nearly parallel to it. A motorist encounters a comparable phenomenon if one front wheel of his car goes off the pavement onto a soft shoulder; the deep earth will slow the wheel down with the result that the other front wheel will outrun it and the car tend to veer around to face the side of the highway. In the case of sea waves, the more resistant medium is the shallower water inshore. Entering at an angle the zone in which the bottom retards them, waves are brought around to strike the shore in near parallel with it. They tend to bear directly down upon it, regardless of their initial direction or the shape of the coast.

Since waves are concentrated on headlands and compressed as they converge on them, it follows that waves entering bays are extended and lose energy as they progress. Any material they pick up as breakers tends to be deposited as their vigor diminishes, and this includes the detritus of the battered headlands. Along a cliff-formed shore, what beaches there are—and they may be of boulders, cobbles, or sand—form in the quieter recesses. By wearing back the promontories and filling in between them the sea works to even out a coast.

If, barring a general uplift of the land, the sternest rockbound shore must yield, what must the consequences then be for lands that breast the seas behind mere earthworks? Such is the plight of the glacially formed outriders of our northeastern coast. Myron G. Fuller of the Geological Survey has estimated that Long Island has lost half its substance to the sea since the ice sheet departed from it. And Long Island is considerably less exposed to the heavier seas than Cape Cod and Nantucket. The plateau built up between two lobes of the glacier that constitutes the forearm of the Cape lies broadside to the easterlies and is being cut back at a rate of more than three feet a year. Unless the rate was lower to begin with, it must have been narrowed by more than six miles in the past ten thousand years. The forearm seems unlikely to last more than another five thousand years, with Nantucket's prospects commensurate and Martha's Vineyard's only somewhat better. It puts one in a queasy and unquiet state of mind to think of it as one walks along the outer Cape's Great Beach, as Thoreau named it, below the cliff that stares off across the sea with frowning imperturbability while the interminable procession of waves marching upon it are working its finish.

If lower and narrower than it once was, the outer Cape is also far longer. The sands of which the sea has despoiled the cliff have been carried north and south. In one direction they account for the upper ten miles of the forearm, ending in the curled spit, like a half-open fist, at Provincetown. In the other they have created two successive spits with a combined length of twenty-five miles—Nauset Beach and Monomoy Island. But most have gone into the vast shoals stretching a hundred miles to the south-

east in which ships past reckoning lie buried.

The sand of the northeastern shores probably originated mostly in glacial till, that of others elsewhere from the erosion of mountains and sandstones of the coastal plain and the interior lowlands. Ranks and files of mountains had to be reared and ground down to produce these oceans of quartz and feldspar grains, peppered with the black grains of rutile, ilmenite, and magnetite, greenish-grey of glauconite, and rose and amber of garnet. And the quantity is still being added to, as the turbidity of rivers reaching the sea attests. Rivers deposit their load of sand where their flow is halted by the ocean. Bars are formed across the bays into which the rivers empty—the well-known "harbor-mouth" bars. In the quiet waters of the Gulf, deltas are formed. But along the Atlantic and Pacific coasts, it is the fate of most river-borne additions to the volume of sand to be carried away.

Beneath the water, the sand of the beach is in continual process of rearrangement. Every wave shifts the sand within its reach, and the greater the wave, the greater the depth to which it reaches. "Waves change the sand and at the same time the sand is changing the waves," says the oceanographic engineer Willard Bascom. "Even in glass-sided wave channels where an endless number of waves, each exactly the same, can be produced, equilibrium is never reached."

Silt may be carried in suspension by ocean currents for long distances, but the transport of sand requires greater turbulence. It does not require much, for a grain of sand in water is very light (its weight in air minus the weight of an equal volume of water). The Gulf Stream, with its four-knot current, is apparently capable of moving sand along the bottom where its waters are constricted, off Florida. Tidal currents, where they are constricted, also move sand. But waves, which provide by far the most important of the sand-moving marine currents, cannot ordinarily lift sand beyond a depth of about thirty feet, even in storms. Inshore of this depth, the sand may be carried up the beach or down from it. For reasons that can only be guessed at, the heavy seas of winter scour sand from the beach and deposit it in offshore bars, where their backflow loses power, while the lesser waves of summer pick the sand up from the bar and transport it to and up the beach. Thus the beach of one season is apt to be narrow and steep, that of the other, broad and level.

It is the alongshore currents that, moving sand laterally, are the prime architects of alterations of sandy coasts. Even after refraction, waves generally strike the beach not quite head-on; sand grains are likely to be set down by the wash of a breaker a little to the side of where they were picked up. And a quarter-of-an-inch displacement multiplied by eight thousand waves a day comes to almost 170 feet. Waves do not by any means always strike the shore from the same quarter. However, on both our Atlantic and Pacific coasts the prevailing direction of the larger waves and littoral currents is from north to south. The movement of sand down the coast is particularly vigorous in southern California. Joseph Caldwell of the U.S. Army Corps of Engineers has computed that in average weather the energy used to move sand between Point Conception and Los Angeles comes to about five million foot-pounds per foot of beach per day, or five hundred horsepower per mile. The construction of a breakwater at Santa Barbara gave an opportunity to measure what is being moved, for the sand accumulates on the far side of the barrier and periodically has to be removed. The Corps of Engineers has found that on the average between four hundred and nine hundred cubic yards arrive daily.

It is not only artificial breakwaters that cause the waves to unload. Where a shore ends or turns inland, the breakers fan out, losing momentum, and release the sand they have been carrying so as to extend the previous shoreline. Hence the long spits of upper Cape Cod and Nauset Beach, which extend the shoreline of the Great Beach. Where a volume of water regularly rounds the end of a spit, the spit tends to curve with it and form a hook. The hook at Provincetown comes three-quarters of the way around a circle. Sandy Hook is actually three successive hooks; each time a hook has formed, the tendency of the waves to extend the spit straight ahead has prevailed. Willapa Bay, just above the mouth of the Columbia River and Bolinas Lagoon, north of San Francisco, are examples of bays that have become almost cut off from the sea by spits. Another is Pleasant Bay at the elbow of Cape Cod, where the spit is Nauset Beach. In extreme northern California, U.S. 101 goes from one headland to another over spits that have

formed entirely across the mouth of the bays between them. In Nantucket, Martha's Vineyard, outer Long Island, and northern New Jersey indentures in the coast have likewise been wholly sealed off and converted into freshwater lakes.

From Long Island southward, long, narrow sand spits, more often than not detached from the mainland as so-called barrier islands or sand reefs fringe most of our eastern and Gulf coasts, where the offshore gradients are gentle. Seldom more than a mile wide and usually much less, they are bordered on the ocean side by nearly straight, broad beaches and on the landward side by marshes. Fire Island, along the outer shore of Long Island, and Assateague Island, lying athwart the Maryland-Virginia border, each thirty-odd miles long, are good examples of the sand-reef island. Both, like the upper arm of Cape Cod, are in major part now incorporated in the National Park system and hence protected from the invasion of beach cottages to which it is the normal fate of such islands to succumb. Padre Island, a rope of sand over one hundred miles long off the extreme southern coast of Texas, and 125 miles of barrier islands off the North Carolina coast, have also been recently added to the National Park system.

The North Carolina Outer Banks jut into the ocean to a maximum distance of twenty-five miles, at Cape Hatteras. Why they do so and why, southward, there is the broad scalloping of the coast, which is like the edge of a bat's wing, with the fingertips of Cape Hatteras, Cape Lookout, Cape Fear, and Cape Ro-

main, is a subject of speculation. The Gulf Stream, that equivalent of a thousand Mississippis, comes closer to the coast in this sector than anywhere else after rounding Florida, and one theory is that side currents curling off it are responsible for the concavities of the coast. A corollary is that its side effects before it veers away from the continent also cause the littoral currents to relinquish enough of their load of sand at the apex of the banks to have created and to maintain Diamond Shoals. These stretch for some fifteen miles offshore and, lying in wait for ships caught in easterlies, have made Hatteras a byword for disaster at sea.

Out of sight of land as they are, mostly low-lying and attenuated, perpetually assailed by gnashing breakers, the Outer Banks—Hatteras and Ocracoke islands—raise insistently the question of why there should be barrier islands at all, anywhere. On Long Island, beginning at Montauk Point and working westward, one witnesses a complete gradation from beaches that are part of the main body of the land, to beaches that enclose former indentures of the shore, to beaches that are long spits enclosing large bays, to beaches that are similarly long spits but disconnected. All of them are formed of sand the sea has washed from the retreating end of the moraine at Montauk Point. It would seem that in this evolutionary exhibit there is an explanation of the barrier islands. But whether, in view of their extent, it is a sufficient one is another matter. A well-established school of thought has it that they are bars of the kind formed offshore by winter seas which have become elevated.

The related question has to do with the future of the barrier islands. There seems to be a large measure of agreement, backed by substantial evidence, that they are doomed. This is writ, it is said, partly by their slow creep shoreward, as dunes are rolled inland by onshore winds, and partly by the filling up of the lagoons behind them with river-borne silt and windblown sand. Yet there has been plenty of time since the oceans reached roughly their present level for the two fatal processes to have done their work, or so one would suppose. And there the barrier islands still are.

One factor in the preservation of the lagoons may be the slow subsidence of the southeastern coast, reportedly about a foot a century. Of this, the lesser part (it is uncertain how much) represents the rise of the oceans occasioned by a worldwide warming trend, which is releasing water from the remaining ice sheets. (The trend apparently began in the middle of the eighteenth century, when alpine glaciers generally reached their greatest extent. The warmest period since the last ice age seems to have been about five thousand years ago, when most if not all alpine glaciers probably disappeared and the oceans must have stood six or eight feet higher than at present. A "little ice age" beginning three thousand years ago saw the alpine glaciers restored and the ice sheets expanded again at the expense of the oceans.) The rest of the difference in sea level is accounted for by the actual sinking of the land— a phenomenon one is tempted to relate to the weight of sediments accumulating on the basement granite of the continental shelf, which are

nearly two miles thick at Cape Hatteras and upwards of four miles thick at their maximum.

Whatever their origins or prospects, the barrier islands, it is evident, are being maintained as they are by a remarkably fine balance between the beach-augmenting and the beach-depleting activities of the waves. To keep their backs above water, the islands have two allies. One, albeit a fickle and treacherous one, is the wind, which lifts the sand from the dry upper beach and piles it above the sea's reach.

If it were not known from experience that hills of sand rise behind beaches, they would certainly never be expected to do so. But dunes do form wherever there are broad expanses of loose granules large enough for the wind to get under but small enough for it to lift. Apparently they originate from an irregularity in the surface. Windblown grains pelting a sandy (or otherwise rough) forward slope must tend to lodge there when the wind is not strong enough to lift them over the obstruction; those that just clear it tend to drop behind it owing to the wind's loss of velocity on the leeward side. The dune thus commenced is capable of sustained growth, but the higher it rises the stronger and more damaging the winds that sweep its crest. Forty feet is high for a dune on the East Coast, though dunes much higher are found on upper Cape Cod at Ipswich, Massachusetts, and at Nags Head on the North Carolina Banks. The Oregon Dunes, which are seas of sand occupying a forty-mile stretch of coast north of Coos Bay, rise to two hundred feet. So do those along the southwestern shore of Lake Michigan, which have been piled up by northwest-ers sweeping across the water. (Dunes are, of course, by no means confined to shores. Death Valley has a fine collection. The sands driven by westerlies across the valley of the upper Rio Grande in the most arid part of Colorado have collected against the slopes of the Sangre de Cristo Mountains in dunes measuring up to seven hundred feet high.)

As sand collects just under the brim of a dune the slope grows so steep that a sand-slide takes place. Dunes thus acquire sharp ridge lines and partially concave leeward slopes. They also, through the movement of sand up their faces and over their crests, have the habit of rolling inland. Some, in the course of years or decades, have been known to roll clear across a barrier island and into the lagoon, burying woods and human works on their way and later uncovering their ruins.

The migration of dunes would be far more active than it is but for the second ally of the barrier isles and the sand-coasts in general: plants, which are the stabilizers of the sand. The realm of beach area that plants have invaded is as inhospitable as the desert, and plants' adaptations to the two are similar. Some rely on succulence and a reservoir of fresh water, others on the impermeability of wiry or leathery foliage. Pulpy herbaceous plants pioneer the extreme upper beach and the forward slopes of the front rank of dunes. In the North the dunes are crested with beach-grass, in the South with sea oats. Behind the front rank of dunes spread skeins of bearberry and blankets of beach heather. With them come the first thickets. In the North these are of stiff-twigged bayberry, scraggly beach plum and Asiatic roses, and in the South of sand myrtle (close kin of bayberry), silverling, and yaupon holly. Advancing from the rear come the first trees—the dwarf bear oak in the North, the low-domed live oak in the South, and pines, their species growing taller of stature and longer of leaf from New England through Georgia.

As the dunes are shaped like waves by the winds, so the forward masses of vegetation are shaped like dunes and often sheered smooth as hedges. This is the effect of salt spray, which is fatal to all but the best-defended plant tissues. After an easterly gale, foliage that is hundreds of yards from the surf will exhibit salt-spray "burn," while spray carried by the hurricane winds will destroy foliage miles inland. Even rearward dunes subdued by woods for a generation or more may not be secure. If the vegetative cover is breached, a blowout may occur, releasing the sand to pour forth on a path of destruction. But the plants never give up. Eventually, except where man has upset the natural order, the errant sand will be tamed again.

In the far South, plants are a still more aggressive and effective ally of the land's. On the southwest coast of the Florida peninsula, from the Keys up the Gulf Coast for a distance of 150 miles or so, mangroves stalk out into the sea's shallows. Seedlings dropped from the adult trees drift with the tides and currents until their sharp down-pointed root ends make contact with a spit or bar with which they can engage. Their roots spreading into the sand and silt, the seedlings grow, as do others joining them on the anchorage. With development, roots like upside-down branches arch out from the trunks and from one another, forming a seine which collects sediments and the flotsam of the sea. In time the grove is mired in. Unless a hurricane ravages it, stripping off foliage and bark to expose the underlayers of the trunks and limbs to the lethal salt spray, leaving a ghost forest in its wake, solid ground will be built up beneath it. The coast will be advanced or a new island formed.

Along Florida's southern coasts the temperature of the waters seldom drops below 70 degrees, and then not for long; that means they are suitable for reef-building corals. During the era of mild temperatures between the third and fourth ice ages, when the oceans may have stood a hundred feet higher than they do today and all Florida was submerged but for the extreme northern and some central parts, a line of reefs grew just off the present southeast coast of the peninsula. At the same time, the substructure of the adjacent mainland was being prepared by processes recently elucidated by J. Edward Hoffmeister, who found them at work today in the Bahamas. What is now a ridge of limestone up to twenty-five feet high bordering the Atlantic Coast of the peninsula on the south was a bar formed of limestone granules the size of sand grains deposited directly by seawater supersaturated with calcium carbonate. The present floor of the Everglades was a submerged shelf behind the bar built up by the calcareous shells of marine organisms, mostly by colonies of minute bryozoans or "moss-animals." With the fall of the

The shoreline is the frontier
along which the continents
are under ceaseless attack by
the rhythmically pounding sea.
Battered as well by rain,
gouged by streams and riven by
ice, the continents should
have yielded long ago, it would
seem, and have disappeared
as sediments under a universal
sea, even before life had
gained a foothold on the land.
Yet they have endured, borne
up by forces we are only
now beginning to understand.

ocean's level in the latest ice age, the bar and the bryozoan flats were exposed and solidified by rains depositing calcium carbonate in their pores. The reefs were also exposed and their tiny builders killed. Today these form the upper, or eastern, Keys, which are adjacent to the coast and forested in tropical hardwoods. The Keys of the remainder of the chain, which are directly in line with the first—probably because the chain as a whole parallels the edge of the continental shelf—consist of protrusions of underlying limestone of diverse origin and are pine-clad. And, paralleling the Keys, at the edge of the continental shelf, a new line of reefs is growing, the work of coral polyps, coralline algae, and marine worms.

Thanks to the mangroves and the reefs, tropical Florida may stand to gain substantially at the sea's expense in the course of time. But in the long run, in the absence of a shift to its advantage in the relative level of beach and sea, the land as a whole can only lose in the contest with the covetous medium that tirelessly worries its periphery. A return to the climate of the most recent interglacial age, releasing the six million cubic miles or so of water held in the ice sheets of Antarctica and Greenland, could again raise sea levels by as much as two hundred feet. That would inundate every seaport in the world and send the ocean over coastal plains to the fall line. Conversely, of course, another ice age would bring about the retreat of the ocean and the re-emergence of much of the continental shelves, but only at a heavy cost to the land. The movement of sand along the coasts may extend spits up to a point

and add to the lower end of barrier islands even as it steals from the upper, but like all conveyor belts, this one has an end. Somewhere the moving sand must be lost in the depths. And the process of loss can only be enormously advanced by the landslips that seem to send huge quantities of sand, gravel, and boulders sweeping across the continental shelf and down the slope to the floor of the sea. One such slide off the coast of Newfoundland, timed by its progress in snapping submarine cables, had an initial velocity of sixty miles an hour. These onrushes of sediment-laden waters, "turbidity currents," are suspected of having much to do with the scouring out of the mysterious canyons, some surpassing even the Grand Canyon, that cut across the continental shelf.

Yet the physical world seems to be a system of circuits, in which the end of the cycle is its beginning. Rock, which can only suffer continuing dissolution in the realm of the land (apart from such local and temporary reversals as the conversion of dunes into sandstone) recoups under the confinement of its adversary, on the sea's floor. Where the spoil of the rock is accumulating off Hatteras, there may some day be, high above the water, a sandstone gorge with walls stained red with iron oxide from a ship entombed in the shoals.

Or a mountain range may rise where of all places one seems most unlikely today, along our low-lying Gulf Coast. Half a dozen considerable rivers empty there, discharging their loads of sediment. The greatest by far, the Mississippi, which carries 40 per cent of all the water reaching the sea from the rivers of the

United States, dumps a cubic mile of solids into the Gulf every fifteen years. Not only has it filled in the embayment that once reached southern Illinois, but it has spread a delta out across the continental shelf. All streams emptying in quiet waters form deltas, but the Mississippi's, which has taken shape as the channels have shifted course, is notable in extent as well as in its "bird's foot" configuration. The far greater part, however, is invisible. Drilling has shown that the sedimentary strata of the Gulf coastal plain and of the continental shelf beyond it thicken drastically toward the sea. Cenozoic sediments of the coastal plain have been penetrated to a depth of twenty thousand feet. From there out their bottom is too deep to be reached by a drill. Philip C. King's estimate is that Cenozoic and Mesozoic strata off the coast achieve a thickness of between forty and fifty thousand feet and that the slope of the continental shelf has been advanced during Cenozoic times for several hundred miles. Inasmuch as these deposits were all laid down in a shallow sea, the inference is that the crust has been subsiding beneath them—that they have been filling an ever-deepening trough. Thus the stage is set much as it was for the rise of the Appalachian and Rocky mountains.

Whether mountains will actually rise there is another matter. The land-leveling processes are pretty well understood, but too little is known of those that work to opposite ends to tempt geologists to predict what their course will be. (Why have sediments laid down in the West in the past million years long since solidified into rock while others forming part of the eastern coastal plain remain unchanged after a hundred million?) The mainsprings of the continent-building forces are still mysterious. It would, however, at least seem reasonable to believe that through the creation of new mountains continental growth will, as in the past, certainly do no less than keep pace with continental depletion—for there is some evidence to indicate that the continents are today larger than ever. That this is the prospect would, moreover, appear to follow from the current conjecture that the material of the earth's mantle is in circulation, albeit with an infinitely slow pulse and pace, moving the detritus of the continents from the ocean's floor back into their roots and preparing the crust for the gestation of new mountains. That process, if the hypothesis is sound, must continue until the earth's store of radioactivity is exhausted. Necessarily it will run out, just as the sun's store of nuclear fuel must in time begin to fail. When the sun nears its end some five billion years hence, according to current predictions, it will suffer a monstrous enlargement in which our planet will be incinerated. All stars must burn out.

Yet if the universe is doomed to run down, it can only be, one feels, because it is destined by one means or another for renewal; such is one's faith in the circularity of natural processes, not excluding that of time itself. Until it has been proved wrong one may rest with the conclusion James Hutton reached when, gazing into the depths of the past and of the future, he perceived "no vestige of a beginning, no prospect of an end."

THE NATIONAL "MUSEUMS" OF GEOLOGY

Since 1872 the United States has set aside more than twenty million acres as National Parks and Monuments for the enjoyment of all its citizens. Listed here are those especially noteworthy for what they reveal of the continent's geologic history.

In addition, seven National Seashores—Cape Cod, Fire Island, Assateague, Cape Hatteras, and Cape Lookout on the Atlantic; Padre Island on the Gulf of Mexico; Point Reyes on the Pacific—offer the spectacle of the great geologic force, the sea, at work.

Further information about any Park or Monument may be obtained by writing to its superintendent, at the address given.

ACADIA NATIONAL PARK
Box 338, Bar Harbor, Maine 04609
Before the ice age, Mount Desert Range was an unbroken ridge of pink granite; when the ice retreated, a line of individual summits, separated by deep valleys, emerged scarred and polished and only a portion of their former height.

ARCHES NATIONAL MONUMENT
c/o Canyonlanas National Park, Moab, Utah 84532
More than eighty giant arches, windows, and pinnacles have been carved from sandstone by the erosive action of water.

BADLANDS NATIONAL MONUMENT
Box 72, Interior, South Dakota 57750
This forlorn, arid landscape once was a marshy plain hospitable to saber-toothed cats, giant pigs, and dog-sized camels and horses. Their fossils abound in the rocks that date to forty million years ago.

BIG BEND NATIONAL PARK
Big Bend National Park, Texas 79834
Hardened sediments of ancient seas were deformed, thrust upward, and tilted into mountains; the sea advanced again, then retreated, leaving marshes and forests in the era of the dinosaur; more activity created new mountains. Water has carved deep canyons in the area, revealing in profile the chapters of this geologic history, spanning millions of years.

BLACK CANYON OF THE GUNNISON NATIONAL MONUMENT
c/o Curecanti Recreation Area, 334 South 10th St., Montrose, Colorado 81401
The Gunnison River has cut a canyon to a depth of almost twenty-five hundred feet, down through sedimentary rocks and old volcanic flows to a Precambrian floor of granite, gneiss, and schist.

BRYCE CANYON NATIONAL PARK
Bryce Canyon, Utah 84717
"The stunningest thing out of a picture," said one of the canyon's first surveyors. In rich autumnal colors, the strata that form the walls of Bryce Canyon were deposited within the last sixty million years; the canyon's rocks are younger than those of neighboring Zion Canyon and of the Grand Canyon.

CANYONLANDS NATIONAL PARK
Moab, Utah 84532
Among the weird formations and geologic mysteries in this recently acquired park is Upheaval Dome, a conical structure two miles wide at the base with a crater forty-five hundred feet across and sixteen hundred feet deep. It resembles a volcano in form and color, yet is sedimentary in origin.

CAPITOL REEF NATIONAL MONUMENT
Torrey, Utah 84775
The rocks of this area were buckled and folded about sixty million years ago; subsequent erosion created deep gorges along the fractures as well as innumerable towers, pinnacles, and domes.

CAPULIN MOUNTAIN NATIONAL MONUMENT
Capulin, New Mexico 88414
An active volcano about seven thousand years ago, Capulin Mountain rises a thousand feet above the plain; it is one of the largest and most symmetrical of the geologically recent cinder cones in the United States.

CARLSBAD CAVERNS NATIONAL PARK
Box 1598, Carlsbad, New Mexico 88220
In limestone formed from inland-sea deposits about 250 million years ago, acidified groundwater widened hairline cracks into ever-larger cavities; as the water table was lowered over a period of thousands of centuries, the chambers were drained and the dissolving process moved deeper into the earth. The lowest of the magnificent Carlsbad caves are 850 feet below ground. Other limestone caverns in the West, all of smaller size, are *Lehman Caves* in Nevada, *Oregon Caves* near the California border, *Timpanogos Cave* in Utah, and *Jewel Cave* and *Wind Cave* in South Dakota.

CEDAR BREAKS NATIONAL MONUMENT
c/o Zion National Park, Springdale, Utah 84767
A wide canyon, described as an amphitheater, Cedar Breaks exposes layer upon layer of limestone, ranging in hue from white through yellow and red to lavender, representing deposits in a shallow lake more than fifty million years ago.

CHIRICAHUA NATIONAL MONUMENT
Dos Cabezas Star Route, Willcox, Arizona 85643
The landscape is crowded with slender spires of rock, the remnants of lava masses that were cracked during an uplift and then eaten away by erosion.

COLORADO NATIONAL MONUMENT
c/o Curecanti Recreation Area, 334 South 10th St., Montrose, Colorado 81401
Sixty million years ago, as the Rocky Mountains were being formed, this area was lifted above the surrounding countryside and a crack in the crust produced a fault ten miles long. Erosion has produced canyons that reveal rocks back to the Precambrian; the fault is still revealed in a long cliff hundreds of feet high.

CRATER LAKE NATIONAL PARK
Box 7, Crater Lake, Oregon 97604
This beautiful blue lake occupies the crater of a volcano that was active less than seven thousand years ago. The peak collapsed; there are competing theories why. Now its low-lying rim encompasses a receptacle for rain and snow five miles in diameter and more than nineteen hundred feet deep.

CRATERS OF THE MOON NATIONAL MONUMENT
Box 29, Arco, Idaho 83213
Along a zone of weakness in the earth's crust, lava has produced a weird and varied display of volcanic phenomena: cinder cones, craters, frozen lava flows, volcanic bombs, and caves. Eruptions occurred at least as recently as sixteen hundred years ago.

DEATH VALLEY NATIONAL MONUMENT
Death Valley, California 92328
Rocks from every era of geologic history are revealed in the valley and its bordering mountains, in a varied landscape created by all the great geologic forces: water, wind, volcanism, the faulting and folding of great land masses. The lowest spot on the continent, 280 feet below sea level, is only eighty miles from Mount Whitney, the highest point (at 14,495 feet) in the forty-eight states.

DEVILS POSTPILE NATIONAL MONUMENT
Box 577, Yosemite National Park, California 95389
Worth a side trip from Yosemite National Park, the Devils Postpile is a hunk of basalt that cracked into slender three- to seven-sided columns as it cooled. Glacial ice tore most of it apart, but left a remnant two hundred feet high.

DEVILS TOWER NATIONAL MONUMENT
Devils Tower, Wyoming 82714
Similar in origin but far more impressive than the Postpile is Devils Tower. The round cluster of slender columns is broad at the base, then curves inward and upward to a total height of 865 feet; the visual effect is of a gigantic sawed-off tree trunk.

DINOSAUR NATIONAL MONUMENT
Dinosaur, Colorado 81610
A sandbar in a stream bed, geologists speculate, trapped drowned animals 140 million years ago; the processes of uplift and erosion have brought the petrified skeletons of these animals—principally dinosaurs, crocodiles, and turtles—from deep burial to the surface and human view.

GLACIER BAY NATIONAL MONUMENT
Box 1781, Juneau, Alaska 99801
Over twenty tremendous glaciers—some advancing, others dying—fill the spaces between the magnificent peaks of two parallel mountain ranges. Some face into Glacier Bay; others extend to the ocean, ending in cliffs several hundred feet high.

GLACIER NATIONAL PARK
West Glacier, Montana 59936
A great disturbance called the Lewis overthrust displaced some of the oldest sedimentary rocks on

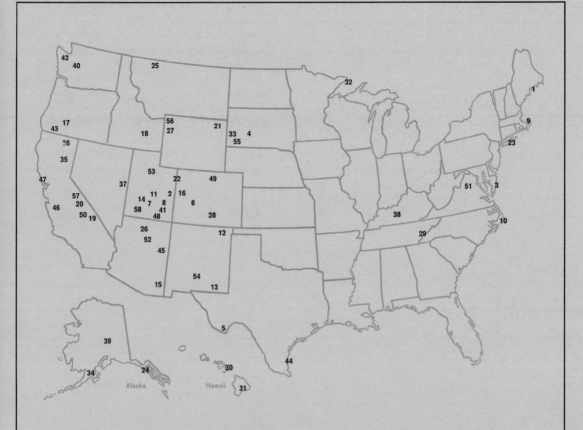

THE RECOMMENDED NATIONAL PARKS, MONUMENTS, AND SEASHORES

1 Acadia N.P., Me.
2 Arches N.M., Utah
3 Assateague Island N.S., Md.-Va.
4 Badlands N.M., S. Dak.
5 Big Bend N.P., Tex.
6 Black Canyon of the Gunnison N.M., Colo.
7 Bryce Canyon N.P., Utah
8 Canyonlands N.P., Utah
9 Cape Cod N.S., Mass.
10 Cape Hatteras N.S., N.C.
11 Capitol Reef N.M., Utah
12 Capulin Mountain N.M., N. Mex.
13 Carlsbad Caverns N.P., N. Mex.
14 Cedar Breaks N.M., Utah
15 Chiricahua N.M., Ariz.
16 Colorado N.M., Colo.
17 Crater Lake N.P., Oreg.
18 Craters of the Moon N.M., Idaho
19 Death Valley N.M., Calif.-Nev.
20 Devils Postpile N.M., Calif.

21 Devils Tower N.M., Wyo.
22 Dinosaur N.M., Utah-Colo.
23 Fire Island N.S., N.Y.
24 Glacier Bay N.M., Alaska
25 Glacier N.P., Mont.
26 Grand Canyon N.P., Ariz.
27 Grand Teton N.P., Wyo.
28 Great Sand Dunes N.M., Colo.
29 Great Smoky Mountains N.P., N.C.-Tenn.
30 Haleakala N.P., Hawaii
31 Hawaii Volcanoes N.P., Hawaii
32 Isle Royale N.P., Mich.
33 Jewel Cave N.M., S. Dak.
34 Katmai N.M., Alaska
35 Lassen Volcanic N.P., Calif.
36 Lava Beds N.M., Calif.
37 Lehman Caves N.M., Nev.
38 Mammoth Cave N.P., Ky.
39 Mount McKinley N.P., Alaska
40 Mount Rainier N.P., Wash.

41 Natural Bridges N.M., Utah
42 Olympic N.P., Wash.
43 Oregon Caves N.M., Oreg.
44 Padre Island N.S., Tex.
45 Petrified Forest N.P., Ariz.
46 Pinnacles N.M., Calif.
47 Point Reyes N.S., Calif.
48 Rainbow Bridge N.M., Utah
49 Rocky Mountain N.P., Colo.
50 Sequoia N.P. and Kings Canyon N.P., Calif.
51 Shenandoah N.P., Va.
52 Sunset Crater N.M., Ariz.
53 Timpanogos Cave N.M., Utah
54 White Sands N.M., N. Mex.
55 Wind Cave N.P., S. Dak.
56 Yellowstone N.P., Wyo.-Mont.-Idaho
57 Yosemite N.P., Calif.
58 Zion N.P., Utah

earth, sending them on top of much younger rocks. Valleys were cut, first by stream erosion, later—a million years ago—by great glaciers. A few puny glaciers lie along the paths carved by the great ones.

GRAND CANYON NATIONAL PARK
Box 129, Grand Canyon, Arizona 86023
Over a nine-million-year period the Colorado River has cut a mile-deep canyon through rocks spanning nearly two billion years of geologic history; the bottommost cut, called the Inner Gorge, is a narrow wedge through Precambrian schist. The view from the rim has been called "the greatest visual shock a human being can experience."

GRAND TETON NATIONAL PARK
Box 67, Moose, Wyoming 83012
The jagged, spectacular Grand Tetons are a classic example of mountains created of a fault-block. The eastern face rises steeply from the plains; the western slope is far more gradual. Here also is a landscape carved by mountain streams and glaciers.

GREAT SAND DUNES NATIONAL MONUMENT
Box 60, Alamosa, Colorado 81101
The San Luis Valley, three times the size of Delaware, is a reminder that not all the sand is of the sea. The shifting desert dunes, some more than seven hundred feet high, are composed of material swept down from neighboring mountains.

GREAT SMOKY MOUNTAINS NATIONAL PARK
Gatlinburg, Tennessee 37738
Only an occasional hole in the thick carpet of vegetation reveals the twisted striations of very ancient sediments uplifted some two hundred million years ago. The Great Smokies remained among the loftiest of the Appalachian Range, lying safely south of the great ice flows of the Pleistocene.

HALEAKALA NATIONAL PARK
Box 456, Kahului, Maui, Hawaii 96732
A volcano began on the ocean's floor millions of years ago, built upon itself and emerged from the sea to a height of nearly twelve thousand feet, then lay quiet as the forces of erosion took over. A more recent period of activity—which may not yet be finished—resulted in eruptions in the 1790's.

HAWAII VOLCANOES NATIONAL PARK
Hawaii Volcanoes National Park, Hawaii 96718
The geologic history resembles that of Haleakala, but the added attraction here is that the volcanoes are still active. Kilauea erupted in 1967; an eruption in 1959 sent brilliant fountains of lava skyward, one as high as nineteen hundred feet.

ISLE ROYALE NATIONAL PARK
87 North Ripley Street, Houghton, Michigan 49931
This island, the largest in Lake Superior, is composed of Precambrian lava flows interbedded with sandstone and conglomerate. Along its 45-mile length can be found glaciated rocks, as well as gravels from earlier, higher shorelines of the lake.

KATMAI NATIONAL MONUMENT
c/o Mount McKinley National Park
McKinley Park, Alaska 99755
In 1912 an eruption here sent volcanic ash flowing across forty square miles to a depth exceeding four hundred feet. Gas vents in this deposit gave off steam and other vapors, and the place was named the Valley of Ten Thousand Smokes. Today most of these smokes are extinct.

LASSEN VOLCANIC NATIONAL PARK
Mineral, California 96063
Lassen Peak and several of its neighbors are volcanic mountains of the "plug dome" sort. Lassen has been asleep for half a century, but the restless hot springs and steam vents in the area indicate the sleep may not be a permanent one.

LAVA BEDS NATIONAL MONUMENT
Box 867, Tulelake, California 96134
Like the Craters of the Moon, Lava Beds National Monument is a museum of volcanic phenomena: cinder cones, spatter cones, and lava tubes of pahoehoe, the ropy lava that flowed from deep cracks.

MAMMOTH CAVE NATIONAL PARK
Mammoth Cave, Kentucky 42259
In this, one of the great limestone caverns, 150 miles of underground passages have been explored. Unlike Carlsbad, the water table has not fallen below cave level, and the subterranean streams still flow quietly through it, 360 feet below ground.

MOUNT McKINLEY NATIONAL PARK
McKinley Park, Alaska 99755
Mount McKinley, at 20,320 feet, is the highest peak in North America; it is part of the Alaska Range, whose peaks achieved their height in relatively recent geologic time and have suffered little erosion. From McKinley's high slopes, however, come the snows that feed glaciers carving valleys around it.

MOUNT RAINIER NATIONAL PARK
Longmire, Washington 98397
At 14,410 feet, Mount Rainier is the highest and grandest of the West's volcanic peaks. A cap of glacial ice now exists where lava spewed as recently as two thousand years ago.

NATURAL BRIDGES NATIONAL MONUMENT

c/o Canyonlands National Park, Moab, Utah 84532

Three arches, each more than one hundred feet high, are rock spans that were undercut by a stream. Originally they were solid walls of sandstone which the twisting stream wound around, but in making the turn the silt-laden waters gradually scraped through the walls and opened up short-cuts.

OLYMPIC NATIONAL PARK

600 East Park Ave., Port Angeles, Washington 98362

The Olympic Mountains are of sedimentary rock and lava, uplifted to form peaks among the highest of the Coast Ranges. Heavy precipitation feeds the sixty small glaciers in the area that are reminders of the forces that carved the rugged landscape.

PETRIFIED FOREST NATIONAL PARK

Holbrook, Arizona 86025

The colorful, often jeweled logs are the petrified remains of forests that grew on hills above a marshy lowland 200 million years ago. Flowing water rich in silica performed the alchemy that preserved these remarkable specimens.

PINNACLES NATIONAL MONUMENT

Paicines, California 95043

Thirty million years ago a volcanic mountain stood perhaps eight thousand feet high. Faulting of the earth's crust depressed and deformed the mountain, and subsequent tilting, quaking, and erosion completed a landscape of tall rock spires, numerous caves, and a variety of volcanic features.

RAINBOW BRIDGE NATIONAL MONUMENT

c/o Glen Canyon Recreation Area
Box 1507, Page, Arizona 86040

The same process that created the nearby Natural Bridges created this, the largest natural bridge in the world. The imposing Capitol in Washington, D.C., would fit beneath it.

ROCKY MOUNTAIN NATIONAL PARK

Box 1080, Estes Park, Colorado 80517

The complicated history of the Rockies—the seas of a hundred million years ago, the first buckling and breaking, the more recent uplift, the erosion and volcanic activity—can be read amid the peaks and valleys of the Front Range, along the eastern edge of the Rockies.

SEQUOIA NATIONAL PARK

Three Rivers, California 93271

Everything here, and in adjoining Kings Canyon National Park, is on a gigantic scale: the magnificent Sierra Nevada (including Mount Whitney, the highest U.S. peak outside of Alaska); Kings Canyon, the continent's deepest; the Sequoias, the world's largest trees. The Sierras were uplifted and tilted westward in several major stages; the canyons were cut by river flows accelerated by mountain-building activity and by ice age glaciers.

SHENANDOAH NATIONAL PARK

Box 387, Luray, Virginia 22835

Like most of the Appalachian Ranges, the Blue Ridge Mountains hide their origins—in this case, rocks overlain with sediments and lying on a basement of still older granite—under thick foliage.

SUNSET CRATER NATIONAL MONUMENT

c/o Wupatki National Monument
Tuba Star Route, Flagstaff, Arizona 86001

The last eruption in the San Francisco Peaks Volcanic Field occurred in A.D. 1065, creating this awesome cinder cone and sending Indians fleeing.

WHITE SANDS NATIONAL MONUMENT

Box 458, Alamogordo, New Mexico 88310

The Tularosa Basin, the world's largest gypsum desert, is a 100-mile valley of sand dunes and alkali flats. Its gypsum comes from the slopes of two parallel mountain ranges.

YELLOWSTONE NATIONAL PARK

Yellowstone National Park, Wyoming 83020

Nearly surrounded by mountains is an elevated volcanic plateau; the thousands of geysers, hot springs, steam vents, and mud pots are reminders that not far below the surface the earth is still hot. The geysers are famous; less well-known are the spectacular falls and canyon, and the unusual petrified forest in which lava repeatedly surrounded trees and preserved them still upright.

YOSEMITE NATIONAL PARK

Yosemite National Park, California 95389

The tilting and down-faulting of the Sierra Nevadas reached their climax in relatively recent time, hence the very rugged, awesome landscape. But in the cliffs and glacially carved valleys can be read the record of earlier activity—ancient sedimentation, successive uplifts and erosion, and volcanic activity.

ZION NATIONAL PARK

Springlake, Utah 84767

About thirteen million years ago, the deep sedimentary layers of the Zion area began a gradual uplift of thousands of feet, resulting in faults and tilting and the acceleration of stream erosion. Together the processes unearthed sediments almost as old as those of the Grand Canyon and altogether as colorful.

CHRONOLOGY

PRECAMBRIAN

Beginning with the birth of the planet and ending with the advent of an abundant fossil record, this period represents by far the longest and the least understood geologic time span. The earth's crust was formed. Then, through processes unknown, shallow seas and small continental landmasses appeared. North America's oldest known rocks, today exposed in the Canadian Shield, date from this period. The first life appeared: algae-like and fungi-like plants, and soft-bodied marine animals.

PALEOZOIC

CAMBRIAN *Continental-length troughs, on the east and west sides of North America, lay under seas and filled with sediments. These were later to give rise to the Appalachian and Rocky mountains. Seas spread over the continental platform, submerging most of the East and large parts of the Southwest. The sediments that resulted provide the first abundant record of marine life: trilobites, brachiopods, sponges, and other invertebrate creatures.*

ORDOVICIAN *In the greatest flooding of North America in Paleozoic time, more than half of the continent lay under shallow seas. Then the eastern landmass began to rise, and local mountain-building in New England caused the seas to retreat. Invertebrate*

sea life continued to predominate, but the Ordovician period also witnessed the entrance of the first vertebrates—fishes.

SILURIAN *The eastern landmass was emergent long enough to be eroded and planed down before it was again depressed beneath the seas. Primitive plants appeared on land, while new scorpion-like creatures roamed the sea floor. Corals diversified and multiplied in profusion to form extensive coral reefs.*

DEVONIAN *The two troughs and parts of the interior were under water for most of this period. Toward its end, however, mountain-building from southeastern Canada to North Carolina was under way. The close of the Devonian was marked by a general emergence of the continent.*

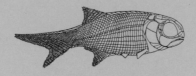

Referred to as The Age of Fishes, this was the first time that vertebrates occupied a prominent position among living forms. Sharks and bony fish were among the advanced forms that appeared. The great transition from water to land was accomplished with the evolution of salamander-like amphibians. Giant tree ferns were present on the land.

MISSISSIPPIAN *Once more the continent was extensively invaded by the sea. Warm water teeming with marine life covered the central interior and limestone deposits over two thousand feet thick were put down. Winged insects appeared.*

PENNSYLVANIAN *Large, primitive trees and ferns crowded vast, swampy lowlands in the eastern part of the continent between recurrent invasions by the sea. (Their buried remains are the origin of the coal fields of the Appalachian Plateaus and the Middle West.) Scorpions, spiders, dragonflies, and cockroaches swarmed the forests. Reptiles appeared.*

PERMIAN *In the East, the Appalachian mountain system reached its apex after a time of intense mountain-building. The West was still covered by shallow seas. A cooler and drier climate caused the extinction of many varieties of plants and animals. Vertebrates—amphibians and reptiles—were numerous.*

MESOZOIC

TRIASSIC *Erosion of the Appalachians spread sediments over the interior lowlands and the still-submerged coastal plain to the east and south. The crustal rocks on the eastern side of the Appalachians were subjected to faulting and tilting with*

GEOLOGIC TIME SCALE

	ERA	PERIOD	EPOCH
	CENOZOIC	QUATER-NARY	RECENT
			PLEISTOCENE
		TERTIARY	PLIOCENE
			MIOCENE
			OLIGOCENE
			EOCENE
			PALEOCENE
100	MESOZOIC	CRETACEOUS	
		JURASSIC	
200		TRIASSIC	
	PALEOZOIC	PERMIAN	
300		CARBON-IFEROUS	PENNSYL-VANIAN
			MISSIS-SIPPIAN
		DEVONIAN	
400		SILURIAN	
		ORDOVICIAN	
500			
		CAMBRIAN	
600	PRECAMBRIAN		

MILLIONS OF YEARS AGO

accompanying intrusions of basaltic magma, of which the Palisades along the Hudson River are a product. Vertebrate animals began to predominate, giving to the entire Mesozoic era its sobriquet, The Age of Reptiles.

JURASSIC In the West, a landmass of high hills roughly covering Idaho, Nevada, Arizona, and southern California contributed sediments to seas on both sides. Late in the period, crustal deformations, with accompanying igneous intrusions, thrust up the western Rocky Mountains from Baja California to Alaska, of which those below Washington and Idaho were later to be drastically altered. Soaring reptiles, birds, and small primitive mammals appeared. Dinosaurs reached the peak of their development. Cycads, resembling modern palms, were also prevalent.

CRETACEOUS The latest and greatest marine invasion of North America since Ordovician time occurred, flooding the western half of the continent. In a series of mighty mountain-making events that continued into the Cenozoic,

sediments from the ancient Cordilleran trough, lying inland of the western Rocky Mountains, were folded and thrust up to form the sedimentary Rockies extending from Alaska to Mexico. Flowering plants became common; dinosaurs became extinct.

CENOZOIC

TERTIARY Considerable activity in the West created new mountain ranges and volcanic peaks, altered the Rockies (creating the Sierra Nevada), and carved the great canyons of the Southwest. Most of the Atlantic and Gulf coastal plains emerged from the sea. By the end of the period the general outlines of the present-day landscape were visible. Mammals replaced reptiles as the predominant representatives of the animal kingdom. Whales and early horses, among others, appeared. Grasslands were extensive.

QUATERNARY Four major glaciations occurred over much of North America, putting the finishing touches on the surface of our present-day landscape. In the Northwest a line of volcanoes arose along the Cascade Range. Mammals continued to predominate and became more varied. Not until one and a half million years ago did early man appear, and evidently did not reach North America until considerably after that time.

151

GLOSSARY OF TERMS

AA A hardened lava stream with a blocky surface. Contrast with *pahoehoe*.

ALLUVIUM A deposit of gravel, clay, silt, or other loose material left by running water, usually on the floodplains of streams and usually in recent geologic time.

ANDESITE A greyish extrusive rock composed mainly of silica, intermediate in composition between basalt and rhyolite.

ANTECEDENT STREAM A river that cut through a barrier as rapidly as the barrier was being formed and thus has kept its original course.

ANTICLINE Upfolded rock layers. An anticline always has its oldest rock layers in its center.

ARCHIPELAGO Any sea or other expanse of water having many scattered islands; also, the islands themselves.

BASALT A dark grey igneous rock, the most abundant volcanic rock.

BASIN An area in which the strata slope inward toward the center from all sides; also, an area drained by a river and its tributaries.

BATHOLITH A great mass of deeply intruded, igneous rock, usually dome-shaped and extending downward to unknown depths.

BRECCIA Rock formed by the solidification of angular fragments of pre-existing rocks.

BUTTE A steep-sided isolated hill with a flat top, formed by erosion around the resistant cap rock. Generally a butte is smaller than a *mesa*.

CALDERA A very large cavity at the top of a volcano, its size owing either to a collapse of the central part of the volcano or to an extraordinarily powerful volcanic explosion.

CEMENTATION The process by which loose deposits of sand, silt, or gravel become hard rock by the addition of some waterborne cementing material, such as calcite.

CIRQUE A bowl-shaped basin cut into the side of a mountain by glacial erosion.

COLUMNAR JOINTING Parallel, vertical cleavages in rock, usually in basaltic lava.

CONGLOMERATE A rock formed by the cementation of rounded rock fragments, commonly of various sizes.

CONTINENTAL SHELF The gently sloping plain at sea bottom that borders nearly every continent. Its seaward limit is generally taken to be one hundred fathoms deep and is often marked by a steep slope.

CORAL REEF A chain or range of rocks composed mainly of fragments of corals, coral sands, and shells of other organisms.

CORDILLERA A great mountain chain or ridge; in the United States, the mountainous region between the Central Plains and the Pacific Ocean, embracing the Rocky Mountains, Sierra Nevada, Cascade Mountains, and other ranges.

DETRITUS Material produced by the wearing away of exposed surfaces; debris.

DIATOMITE A chalk-like sedimentary rock composed chiefly of the siliceous remains of microscopic algae (diatoms).

DIKE A tabular body of igneous rock which has intruded (usually vertically) other rocks.

DIORITE A granular, intrusive igneous rock similar to granite, only much darker.

DRIFT Rock material that has been transported and deposited by glacial movement.

DRUMLIN A low hill of elliptical or elongated shape, composed of glacial debris.

ERRATIC A rock carried some distance from its original bed by a glacier.

ESCARPMENT A steep inland cliff resulting from faulting or the erosion of strata.

ESKER A narrow ridge of sandy or gravelly material formed by a stream flowing beneath a continental glacier.

FAULT A fracture in the earth's crust accompanied by the displacement of the rocks on one side relative to the rocks on the other side. The fracture creates an inclined plane: in a *normal fault* the rocks on one side appear to have slipped down the inclined plane; in a *reverse* or *thrust fault* the rocks on one side appear to have been pushed up the inclined plane; in a *strike-slip fault* the movement has been horizontal.

FIORD A long, narrow coastal inlet with steep walls that were carved by glaciers.

GABBRO A dark intrusive igneous rock that is granitic in texture but basaltic in composition.

GEYSER A hot spring that sporadically shoots up jets of hot water and steam as a result of contact between subterranean water and hot rock.

GNEISS A metamorphic, granite-like rock with thick bands of alternating light- and dark-colored minerals.

GRANITE The plutonic rock of which the continents are chiefly formed, light-colored and with a granular structure and even texture.

GYPSUM A soft sedimentary rock composed of the mineral of the same name, often found in thick beds where a shallow inland sea once existed.

HANGING VALLEY A valley that ends high on the slopes of another valley; especially, a valley that is tributary to a U-shaped glacial trough.

IGNEOUS ROCK Rock formed by the solidification of a molten mass (magma). If the mass flows to the surface, the resulting rock is called *extrusive;* if it flows below the surface among existing rocks, its cooled form is called *intrusive* rock.

ISOSTASY The theory that portions of the earth's crust of low specific gravity tend to stand topographically higher than portions of high specific gravity, other things being equal.

KAME A short ridge or hill of roughly sorted sand or gravel deposited by a glacier.

KARST A honeycombed limestone area characterized by sinkholes and abrupt ridges, often formed below the ground by water action.

LACCOLITH Intruded magma that has pushed the covering sedimentary rock strata into a dome-like shape.

LAGOON A shallow, enclosed salt-water pond or lake, usually very close to a sea.

LAVA Molten rock as it emerges at the surface from a volcano or fissure. Underground it is *magma.*

LIMESTONE A finely grained sedimentary rock consisting largely of calcium carbonate. Limestone is the most extensively used rock in the world, its many varieties ranging in use from blackboard chalk to building stones.

LITTORAL Of or pertaining to a shore, especially of the sea.

LOESS A non-stratified brownish loam deposit of wind-blown dust.

MAGMA Molten rock beneath the earth's surface, called *lava* if it emerges at the surface.

MANTLE That part of the earth's crust beginning about twenty miles beneath its surface and extending about halfway to the earth's center.

MARBLE A metamorphic rock formed by the physical and chemical alteration of limestone or dolomite. Its color patterns and workability make it useful in architecture and ornamentation.

MESA An isolated hill or mountain having sharply sloping sides and a flat top. A small mesa is a *butte.*

METAMORPHIC ROCK A rock formed by physical or chemical changes in pre-existing sedimentary or igneous rock.

MINERAL A crystalline, inorganic substance found in nature and especially in rocks that has a definite chemical composition and definite physical properties.

MORAINE An accumulation of earth and stones deposited by a glacier.

OBSIDIAN A hard igneous rock, black to reddish-brown, glassy in appearance.

OROGENY The process of mountain-building.

OUTCROP That part of a bed of rocks that is exposed at the surface of the earth.

PAHOEHOE Cooled and hardened lava marked by a smooth and often shiny surface. Contrast with *aa.*

PALEONTOLOGY The study of fossil organisms to determine the kinds of life and conditions of past geologic periods.

PALISADE A line of sheer cliffs, especially one resembling a row of columns.

PEGMATITE A coarsely grained igneous rock characterized by an irregularity of grain size, often by huge and beautiful crystals.

PENEPLAIN An "almost plain"; an area from which erosion has removed all prominent irregularities.

PERIOD A division of geologic time, such as Ordovician, Silurian, that is part of an *era* (e.g., Mesozoic) and subdividable into *epochs* (e.g., Eocene, Pleistocene).

PETRIFICATION The process whereby mineral matter, carried by water, replaces the tissues of plants or animals, resulting in a solid replica of the original organic matter.

PLAIN A tract of land having a generally flat or only slightly undulating surface; especially, an area that is treeless.

PLATEAU An elevated tract of land that is comparatively flat.

PLUG DOME A somewhat cylindrical mass of cooled lava occupying the vent of an old volcano.

PLUTONIC ROCK An igneous rock, generally coarse-grained, that has solidified far beneath the earth's surface.

PUMICE An extremely porous rock of volcanic origin.

QUARTZITE A granular and hard metamorphic rock, derived from quartz sandstone.

RHYOLITE A fine-grained, light-colored lava rock with the same mineral content as granite.

SANDSTONE A common sedimentary rock composed of cemented sand grains.

SCHIST A metamorphic rock with thin layers (termed *folia*) containing considerable mica minerals.

SEDIMENTARY ROCK Rock formed by the solidification of sediments. Sedimentary rocks make up about three-fourths of the land area of the world.

SERPENTINITE A lustrous and smooth metamorphic rock, composed mainly of the mineral serpentine, generally of a dark- to light-green mottled color.

SHALE A sedimentary rock formed by the consolidation of mud or clay. It has a finely stratified structure that splits quite easily.

SHIELD The ancient nucleus of a continent, around and upon which younger sedimentary rocks have been deposited.

SILL A tabular mass of igneous rock that has intruded between beds of sedimentary or volcanic rock.

SLATE A common metamorphic rock formed from shale. Unlike shale, its split surface is silky rather than dull.

SPATTER CONE A low steep-sided volcanic cone that results from intermittent spurts of lava from a vent.

SPIT A long, narrow tongue of sand extending from a shore, often running across a bay.

STALACTITE A deposit of crystalline calcium carbonate hanging like an icicle from the ceiling of a cavern.

STALAGMITE Similar to a stalactite, but formed on cavern floors by the steady drip of water saturated with calcium carbonate.

SYNCLINE A trough-like downfold of a stratified rock. A syncline has its youngest rock layers in its center.

TALUS An accumulation of rock debris at the base of a cliff or slope; also, the slope of such a mass.

TECTONIC Pertaining to rock structures resulting from deformation of the earth's crust.

TILL Unstratified, loose glacial drift, consisting of intermingled sand, gravel, and clay. Rock formed from these deposits is called *tillite*.

TUFF A rock composed of small particles thrown from an active volcano, usually in varying degrees of consolidation.

VOLCANO An opening in the surface of the earth from which molten rock, mixed with gases and vapors, flows or is exploded. *Cinder cones* are steep-sided domes with lava fragments surrounding the vent. *Composite cones* are steep-sided domes with alternating layers of volcanic ash, lava flows, and cinders. *Shield volcanoes* are broad and gently sloping, and built almost entirely of lava flows. *Lava domes* generally are steep-sided and built of lava that was pasty and extruded slowly.

FURTHER READING

Asterisk indicates paperback edition.

ROCKS AND MINERALS

Fenton, C.L., and M.A. Fenton. *The Rock Book.* Garden City, New York: Doubleday and Co., Inc., 1940.

Gallant, Roy A., and Christopher J. Schuberth. *Discovering Rocks and Minerals.* Garden City, New York: The Natural History Press, 1967.

Pough, Frederick H. *A Field Guide to Rocks and Minerals.* 3rd ed. Boston: Houghton Mifflin Company, 1955.

THE AMERICAN CONTINENT

Clark, Thomas H., and Colin W. Stearn. *The Geological Evolution of North America.* New York: The Ronald Press Co., 1960.

Farb, Peter. *Face of North America.* New York: Harper & Row, Publishers, 1963.

Ransom, Jay Ellis. *Fossils in America.* New York: Harper & Row, Publishers, 1963.

Shelton, John S. *Geology Illustrated.* San Francisco: W. H. Freeman and Co., 1966.

Shimer, John A. *This Sculptured Earth.* New York: Columbia University Press, 1959.

OF LOCAL INTEREST

Chamberlain, Barbara Blau. *These Fragile Outposts: A Geological Look at Cape Cod, Marthas Vineyard, and Nantucket.* Garden City, New York: The Natural History Press, 1964.

Jaeger, Edmund C. *The North American Deserts.* Stanford: Stanford University Press, 1957.

Krutch, Joseph Wood. *Grand Canyon: Today and All Its Yesterdays.* New York: William Sloane Associates, 1958.

Muir, John. *The Mountains of California.* New York: Doubleday and Co., Inc., 1962.*

Powell, John Wesley. *Exploration of the Colorado River of the West and Its Tributaries.* Garden City, New York: Doubleday and Co., Inc., 1961.*

Thomson, Betty Flanders. *The Changing Face of New England.* New York: The Macmillan Company, 1958.

GENERAL GEOLOGY

Bullard, Fred M. *Volcanoes in History, in Theory, in Eruption.* Austin: University of Texas Press, 1961.

Dunbar, Carl O. *The Earth.* Cleveland: The World Publishing Co., 1966.

Dyson, James L. *The World of Ice.* New York: Alfred A. Knopf, Inc., 1962.

Mather, Kirtley. *The Earth Beneath Us.* New York: Random House, Inc., 1964.

Putnam, William C. *Geology.* New York: Oxford University Press, 1964.

Zumberge, James H. *Elements of Geology.* 2nd ed. New York: John Wiley and Sons, Inc., 1963.

HISTORY OF GEOLOGY

Adams, F.D. *The Birth and Development of the Geological Sciences.* New York: Dover Publications, Inc., 1954.*

Bartlett, Richard A. *Great Surveys of the American West.* Norman: University of Oklahoma Press, 1962.

Fenton, C.L., and M.A. Fenton. *Giants of Geology.* Garden City, New York: Doubleday and Co., Inc., 1952.

Moore, Ruth. *The Earth We Live On.* New York: Alfred A. Knopf, 1956.

THE SHORE

Bascom, Willard. *Waves and Beaches.* Garden City, New York: Doubleday and Co., Inc., 1964.*

Carson, Rachel. *The Edge of the Sea.* Boston: Houghton Mifflin Company, 1955.*

Ogburn, Charlton, Jr. *The Winter Beach.* New York: William Morrow & Company, Inc., 1966.

INDEX

Italics indicate illustrations

A NOTE ON THIS BOOK

This book was published by the Editors of American Heritage Publishing Company in association with the Smithsonian Institution under the following editorial direction: For the Smithsonian Institution, Anders Richter, Director, Smithsonian Institution Press. For American Heritage, Editor, David G. McCullough; Managing Editor, Anthony E. Neville; Art Director, Jack Newman; Assistant Art Director, Donald Longabucco; Copy Editor, Susan M. Shapiro; Assistant Editors, Maria Ealand, Bill Hansen, and Gay Sherry; Picture Editor, Martha F. Grossman; Editorial Assistants, Susan J. Lewis, Nancy Lindemeyer, and Karen Olstad.

PICTURE CREDITS